Opie Percival Read

Judge Elbridge

Opie Percival Read

Judge Elbridge

ISBN/EAN: 9783743305670

Manufactured in Europe, USA, Canada, Australia, Japa

Cover: Foto ©ninafisch / pixelio.de

Manufactured and distributed by brebook publishing software (www.brebook.com)

Opie Percival Read

Judge Elbridge

JUDGE ELBRIDGE.

CHAPTER I.

THE STUDENT AND THE ORATOR.

When John Elbridge retired from the bench, the newspapers said that he had been an honorable judge. He was not a pioneer, but had come to Chicago at a time which we now call an early day, when churches rang their bells where now there is a jungle of trade, when the legs of the Giant of the West were in the ache of "growing pains;" at a time when none but the most visionary dreamed that a mud-hole full of old boots, dead rats, cats, dogs, could ever be worth a million of dollars. Elbridge came from Maryland, with a scant wardrobe, a lawyer's diploma, and the confident ambition of youth. It was not long before he formed a copartnership with a young man named Bodney, a

Kentuckian, in whose mind still lived the chimes of Henry Clay's bells—a memory that not so much fitted him to the law as it atuned him to oratory; but in those days the bar could be eloquent without inviting the pitying smile which means, "Oh, yes, it sounds all right, but it's crude." Elbridge was the student of the firm, and Bodney the orator, not a bad combination in the law at that time, for what one did not know the other was prepared to assert. They prospered in a way, but never had the forethought to invest in the magic mud-hole; took wives unto themselves, and, in the opinion of the "orator," settled down to dull and uneventful honesty. The years, like racing horses, flew round and round the track, and a palace of trade grew out of the mud-hole. Bodney and his wife passed away, leaving two children, a boy and a girl. Elbridge had stood at the bedside of his partner, who was following his wife into the eternal shadow. "Don't worry about the children, Dan; they are mine," said the "student," and the "orator" passed away in peace. And they were his. He took them to his home to be brother and sister to his son; and the years raced round and round the track.

At the time of his retirement from the bench the Judge was asked why he refused longer to serve the people. "Because," said he, "I am beginning to be afraid of my judgment; I am becoming too careful —like the old engineer who can't summon the nerve to bring his train in on time."

Mrs. Elbridge had been known as a local "beauty." It was said that the "orator" had rung his Henry Clay bells for her hand, and with philosophy, a rare quality among orators, had accepted defeat, to spur himself into another contest and to win a woman not unknown to "looks." Rachel Fry, afterward Mrs. Elbridge, had written verses to sky tints and lake hues, and the "student" believed that he had won her with a volume of Keats, bound in blue, the color of one of her own lake odes. And in the reminiscent humor of his older days he was wont to laugh over it until he himself was shot through with a metric thrill, when in measure he strove to recall the past; and then she had the laugh on him. It may be a mere notion, but it seems that the young doctor and the old lawyer are much inclined to write verses, for among the papers of many an aged jurist sonnets are found, and editors are well acquainted with the beguiling smile of the young physician. So the "pink fleece of the cloud-sheep," and the "blue, mysterious soul of the lake," inspirations of the "beauty's" earlier years, found sympathy in the "student's" "mellow morning of sunlit hope," penned in the late afternoon of life. But verses, be they ever so bad, are the marks of refinement, and there was no vulgar streak in the mind of the Judge. His weakness, and he possessed more than one, was the doggedness with which he held to a conviction. His mind was not at all times clear; a neighbor said that he often found himself in a cloud of dust that arose from ancient law books; and it is a fact that an able judge is sometimes a man of strong prejudices. At the time of this narration he was still hale, good humored, a little given to the pedantry of advancing years, devoted to his family, impressive in manner, with his high forehead and thin gray hair; firm of step, heavy in the shoulders, not much above medium height, cleanly shaven, with full lips slightly pouting. Following his own idea of comfort, he had planned his house, a large brick building in Indiana Avenue, at first far out, but now within easy reach of the area where the city's pile-driving heart beats with increasing violence. It was a happy household. The son, Howard, was a manly fellow, studious but wide awake, and upon him the old man rested a precious hope. The mother was a blonde, and nature had given her cast to the boy, blue eyes and yellowish hair; and it was said that if he had a vanity it lay in his bronze beard, which he kept neatly trimmed—and it had come early, this mark of the matured man. His foster brother, George Bodney, was dark, inclined to restlessness, over-impressionable, nervous. The old man had another precious hope—Florence, Bodney's sister; but of this he shall tell in his own words. A stranger might not have seen anything striking about the girl; but all acquaintances thought her handsome. At school she had been called a "character," not that she was original to the degree of being "queer," but because she acted in a manner prematurely old, discussing serious questions with her teachers, debating the problems of life. Her hobby was honor, a virtue which a cynic has declared is more often found among boys than among girls. She liked to read of martyrs, not that there was heaven in their faith, but because she thought it glorious to suffer and to die for a principle, no matter what that principle might happen to be.

There was one other member of the family, William, the Judge's brother. He looked like a caricature of the "student," with thinner hair and thicker lips. He had not given his energies to any one calling; shiftless is the word best fitted to set him forth. He had lived in different parts of the far West, had been dissatisfied with all places because a failure in all, and had come to spend the remainder of his days with his brother in Chicago. Here, he declared, a man could not find disappointment, for no man of sense expected anything but permission to breathe and to keep out of the way. Friends knew that he was the Judge's standing joke, a family laughing stock, a humorous burden, a necessary idleness. Of course, it was natural for him to feel that he owned the place.

Howard and George Bodney were bred to the law, and recently had been admitted to the bar. The "starvation period" of the average young lawyer did not arise out of dull prospect to confront them; they were to make their way, it was true, but they could study and wait. Howard was ambitious, and his mind was grasping. It was said that he "gulped" a book. He did not stop at the stern texts which were to serve as a part of his necessary equipment, but gave himself excursions among those graces of half-idle minds which light a torch for souls that may be greater. He peeped into the odd corners of thought. Once he startled his father by declaring that genius was the unconscious wisdom of ignorance.

THE STUDENT AND THE ORATOR.   11

"It is the reflection of hard work," said the old man. The boy was the corner-stone of his hope; he wanted to feel that his work was to go on, generation after generation, a pardonable vanity, but a vanity nevertheless. He wanted the boy to be practical, for a speculative youth is not a good perpetuator of a father's career. And on one occasion the boy was taken gently to task for reading a decadent book.

"I like to brush up against different minds," said he.

"But nothing is gained by brushing against a diseased mind."

"We might learn something from a mad dog."

"But all of value that we may learn from him," said the old man, "is to keep out of his way. I must request you not to read such books."

Bodney had not distinguished himself. He appeared to be restless and dissatisfied with himself and with his prospects. He thought that the law afforded but a slow and tedious way to make money, and deplored the shortsightedness of his father and his benefactor for not having invested in the mudhole. Nervousness may inspire force of character, but it more often induces weakness. In many respects Bodney was weak. But the Judge, who should have been a shrewd observer of men as well as of principles, did not see it. In the "youth of old age," a man who, in his younger days, may have been keenly of the world, sometimes turns upon life the goggle eye of optimism.

After his retirement from the bench and the more active affairs of the law, the Judge fitted up an office at his home, with desks, long table covered with green baize, books and safe.

One evening Bodney sat alone in the home office, deeply brooding. The household was at dinner, and he heard the hearty laughter of the Judge. He was joking with a guest, a preacher, a good fellow. The young man's brow was dark. Of late he had formed an association with a man named Goyle, clearly an adventurer, but a man to inflame the fancy of a morbid nature. Bodney and Goyle had been much together, at the house and at the office down town, but no one made any objection. Personal freedom was a hobby with the Judge.

There were two doors leading into the office, one opening into a hall, the other into a passageway communicating directly with the street. Through the door opening into the passage Goyle entered. He carried a valise in his hand. Bodney looked up.

"Halloa, Goyle," said he. "Come in."

"Halloa, Goyle," said he. "Come in."

"That's what I'm doing," Goyle replied, putting down the valise near the door and advancing toward the desk at which Bodney was seated.

"Sit down," said Bodney.

"That's what I'm going to do," Goyle replied.

He sat down, and for a time both were silent. "Where's everybody?" Goyle asked.

The bass laughter of the Judge and the contralto of a woman's mirth were heard.

"At dinner," said Bodney, nodding toward the dining room.

"Don't you eat?"

"Sometimes," Bodney answered, and then after a short silence he asked: "Did you get my note?"

"Yes."

"What do you think?"

"I think you're scared," said Goyle.

Bodney gave him a quick look. "Who wouldn't be?"

"I wouldn't."

"Yes, you would. It's this way, and there's no other way to it: The old man has missed money from the safe. He hasn't said so, but I can tell by the way he acts."

Goyle smiled. "Well, but no one but himself

knows the combination of the safe. He doesn't know that you found a piece of paper with the figures on it, does he?"

"Of course not, but it won't be long before he begins to suspect someone."

"Which, necessarily, fastens it on you. Is that it?"

"Doesn't it look like it?"

"Oh, it might," said Goyle. "That is, if you let it?"

Bodney looked at him with reproach. "If I let it. How the duece can I help it? You don't suppose he'd suspect his son Howard, do you? No man could trust a son more than he does."

Goyle shrugged his shoulders. "Didn't trust him with the combination of the safe, did he?"

"No, for it's his idea of business not to trust anyone absolutely. He laughs and jokes all right enough, and says that this is a fine old world, but he hasn't quite forgotten that he practiced law among rascals."

"Yes," said Goyle, leaning back and stretching himself. "This soft air makes me lazy. It's not natural, you know, to be comfortable in Chicago. What were we talking about?"

Bodney turned upon him almost fiercely, but the

visitor looked at him with the self-command of impudent laziness. He was not given to starts. He was born a rascal, and had cultivated his legacy. Coolness may be a virtue; it is also the strongest weapon of the scoundrel, and Goyle was always cool. He motioned with his hand, bowed, smiled, and Bodney's anger was gone.

"Don't get hot, old man," said he. "Everything is all right. If it isn't, we'll make it so. Oh, yes, we were talking about the old gentleman's suspicions. And we've got to take care of them. If I understand it, Howard is to marry your sister. You are all of a family. Your father and the Judge were law partners years ago, and you and your sister were adopted by—"

Bodney waved his hand impatiently. "We know all about that. Yes, and he has been a father to me and I have been—"

"A villain, necessarily," Goyle broke in. "Villainy is born in us, and for a time we may hide out our inheritance, but we can't get away from it. And it's only the weak that struggle against it. The lamb is born with wool and the dog with hair. No, we can't get away from it."

"But we needn't delight in it," said Bodney, with a faint struggle.

"No, and we needn't lie down on it, either. But, to business. The Judge must know who took the money from the safe."

Bodney started. "What, do you think I am going to tell him?"

Goyle yawned. "No, you must show him."

"Show him!"

"Yes. He must see his son Howard take the money."

Bodney stood up and looked down upon him. "Goyle, are you a fool, or do you take me for one? Must see Howard take the money! What do you mean? Do you think I can bribe Howard to take it? I don't understand you."

"Sit down," said Goyle, and Bodney obeyed, looking at him. Goyle lighted a cigarette, turned and pointed to the valise. "The thief is in that grip, and the Judge must see him take the money from the safe. Listen to me a minute. Among my numerous accomplishments I number several failures—one as an actor. But we learn more from a failure than from a success. All right. I heard Howard say that tonight he is going to a reception. In that grip is his semblance—make-up. At the proper time, after Howard is gone, you must lead the Judge in here and see me, as Howard, take money from the safe. On the mother's account the old man can be made to keep quiet—to hold his tongue, and not even say anything to his son. He changes his combination, the affair blows over—and we've got the money."

"Monstrous!" exclaimed Bodney, jumping up and glaring at Goyle.

"Do you think so? Sit down."

Bodney sat down. "Yes, I do think so," he said.

"What, the crime or the—"

"Both. And the trick! Anybody could see through it. It's nonsense, it's rot."

"Yes? Now, let me tell you, Brother Bodney, that life itself is but a trick. The world worships a trick—art, literature, music—all tricks. And what sort of art is the most successful? Bold art. What sort of scoundrel is the most admired by the world? The bold scoundrel. Bold art, my boy."

"But art has its limits and its rules," Bodney feebly protested.

Goyle dropped the stub of his cigarette upon the floor. "Yes, rules for imitators to follow. Originals break rules. Rules are made by weaklings to hamper the success of the strong. You've got to take the right view of life," he said, slowly lifting his hand and slowly letting it drop upon his knee.

"We are living in the nervous atmosphere of adventure and bold trickery. The spirit of this town hates the stagnant; we wipe our muddy feet on tradition. To us the pig squeal of the present is sweeter than the flute of the past. You and I are intellectual failures, and why? The town is against us. Put an advertisement in tomorrow morning's newspaper—'Graduates of Harvard and Yale wanted, fifteen dollars a week,' and see how many answers you'll get. A cartload —and from men who were turned out prepared to fight the battle of life. Think of it. The man who has had his mind trained to failure, whose teaching has made him a refined weakling, with a mind full of quotations and mystic theories— that man has a cause to be avenged upon life, upon society for misleading him. Hear them laughing in there? You don't hear me laughing. I've got nothing to laugh about. You and I know that there isn't any future beyond this infernal life. Then, why hesitate to do anything that works toward our advantage here? I'm talking to your reason now. We have gambled, and we have lost." He turned and shook his finger at the valise. "The thief, I tell you, is in that grip, and he will get us out. If it fails, of course, we are done for, but we are done for if we don't try. I know it's a bold trick, but that's in its favor. It's too bold to be expected or understood. It's no time to think of gratitude. We've got to act. Give me the combination."

They got up, and Bodney stood trembling. He seemed to be struggling to break loose from something that held him in its grasp. Goyle gazed into his eyes. Bodney put up his hand as if to shield them from a dazzling light.

"Give me the combination."

Bodney tore loose from the something that seemed to be gripping him, and started on a run toward the door. Goyle caught him, put his hand on him, held him.

"I hear them coming. Give me that piece of paper."

Bodney gave him a slip of paper. Goyle took up the valise. "Come on," he said, and Bodney followed him out through the door leading into the passage.

CHAPTER II.

THE FAMILY JOKE.

The Judge, his brother William and the Rev. Mr. Bradley entered the office. "Yes, sir," said the Judge, "I'm delighted that you have been called to Chicago. We are full of enterprise here, religious as well as secular. Sit down. And we push religious matters, Mr. Bradley. Here everything takes up the vigorous character of the town. You know that one of our poets has said that when the time comes we'll make culture hum." Bradley sat down, smiling. "Willliam," said the Judge, still standing, "can't you find a chair?"

"Oh, I believe so," William replied, sitting down. "But why do you make everybody sit down and then stand up yourself? Mr. Bradley, my brother John is a browbeater. He forgets that he ain't always on the bench."

The Judge winked at Bradley, and laughed. He was full of good humor, sniffing about on the scent of a prank, and when all other resources failed, he had the reserve fund of his brother, the family joke, the humorous necessity.

"You remember," said Bradley, "I told you, some time ago, that it was my ambition to have a charge here."

The Judge, standing in front of him, began to make convincing motions with his finger, laying down the law, as William termed it. "It's the field, Bradley. You can raise more money in a church here than—"

"Oh, it is not that, Judge," the preacher broke in. "Chicago presents a fertile opportunity for doing good, for making men better, life more worth living, and—"

"Death more certain," William suggested.

"My brother doesn't like it here," said the Judge.

Bradley turned his mild eyes upon the brother and in the form of a question, said, "No?"

William cleared his husky throat. "I have lived further West, where a fellow may make you get out of a stage-coach at the muzzle of a pistol, but he won't sneak up and slip his hand into your pocket."

"My brother took a whirl at the board of trade," said the Judge. He sat down, lighted a cigar, and offered one to Bradley. "Won't you smoke?"

"Not now," Bradley answered. "I am trying to break myself."

"Go down to the board of trade," William suggested. The Judge laughed, and looked as if he were proud of his family joke. "Won't you smoke, William?"

"No," replied the humorous necessity, "I'll wait till I go to my room and then smoke sure enough—a pipe."

"Smoke it here."

"No, I'll put it off—always enjoy it more then. I recollect the tenth of June, sixty-three—was it the tenth or the eleventh? Anyway, a party of us were going—it was the eleventh. Yes, the eleventh. I was only a young fellow at the time, but I liked a pipe, and on that day—no, it must have been the tenth. John, did I say the eleventh?"

"I think you hung a little in favor of the eleventh, William." He winked at Bradley. "And I was sorry to see it, too, for of all the days in June, the tenth is my favorite."

William looked at him and cleared his throat, but the Judge wore the mask of seriousness. The brother proceeded: "Well, I'm reasonably certain it was the tenth. Yes. Well, on the tenth of June, sixty-three, a party of us were going over to—yes, the tenth—over to—"

"Hold on a moment," said the Judge. "Are you quite sure it was the tenth? We want it settled, don't we, Bradley? Of course, you are much younger than we are, Bradley, but you are old enough to enter into the importance of this thing. As far as he can, a preacher should be as exact as a judge." Bradley nodded, laughing, and the flame of William's anger burst forth.

"Confound it, John, don't you suppose I know?"

"I hope so, William," said the Judge.

William snorted. "You don't do anything of the sort, and you know it."

"Well, if I don't I know it, of course, but—"

"Oh, you be confound. You are all the time—"

"Go ahead with your story."

"I'll do nothing of the sort, sir; I'll do nothing of the sort. You are all the time trying to put it on me, and I'll do nothing of the sort; and the first thing you know, I'll pick up and leave here. I was simply going to tell of something that took place on the—Mr. Bradley, did I say the tenth?"

The preacher had not been able to keep a straight face, but with reasonable gravity he managed to say that the tenth was the final date agreed upon. "By all parties concerned," said the Judge, puffing at his cigar. William scratched his head. "But, after all, it must have been on the eleventh."

"Knocks out my favorite again," the Judge muttered, but William took no notice of the interruption. It is the duty of a family joke to be forbearing.

"Ab Tollivar came to me on that day," William began, "and said that there was to be—"

"On the tenth—came to you on the tenth?" the Judge broke in.

"I said the eleventh."

"William, I beg your pardon," the Judge replied, "but you said the tenth, raising my hopes, for you well know my predilection for that day. In many ways a man may be pardoned for recklessness, but not in the matter of a date. The exact time of an occurrence is almost as important as the occurrence itself. History would lose much of its value if the dates—"

"John, when you get into one of your tantrums you are enough to make a snow man melt himself with an oath. You'd make a dog swear."

"Not before me when I was on the bench. But your story. Ab Tollivar came to you and—"

"I'll not tell it." He got up and glared at the

Judge. Oughtn't I to know what day it was on?"

"Yes, and I believe you do. Sit down."

"I'll do nothing of the sort, sir. I'll not sit here to be insulted by you or anybody else." He moved off toward the door, but before going out, halted, turned, and said: "Mr. Bradley, I'll tell you the story some other time. But John shall never hear it." He gave his head a jerk, intended for a bow of indignation, and strode out.

"He's the dearest old fellow in the world," said the Judge, "and I couldn't get along without him."

"Isn't he somewhat younger than yourself?"

"Yes, two years. Come in."

Mrs. Elbridge entered the dingy room, brightening it with her presence. "Won't you please come into the drawing room?" she said. "It is so dreary in here. Judge, why do you bring visitors to this room? After the Judge retired from the bench, Mr. Bradley, he decided to move the main branch of his law office out here, and I didn't think that he would make it his home, but he has; and, worse than that, he makes it a home for all his clients. They can stroll in from the street at any time."

"A sort of old shoe that fits everybody," said the Judge. "The only way to live is to be comfortable, and the only place in which to find comfort is in a room where nothing can be spoiled."

"But won't you please come into the drawing room?"

"Yes, my dear, as soon as I am done smoking."

"But you may smoke in there. Do come, please. The girls want to see Mr. Bradley. Won't you make him come?" she asked, appealing to the preacher.

"Yes, very shortly," replied Bradley. "If he doesn't drop his cigar pretty soon we'll have him driven out with Mr. William's pipe."

"The threat is surely dark enough," she rejoined. "Don't be long, Judge," she added, turning to go. "Agnes declares that you shall not drag Mr. Bradley into your den and keep him shut out from civilized life."

Agnes was a Miss Temple, a visitor, bright and full of mischief. And during all the talk the preacher's mind had been dwelling upon her, the mischief in her eyes and the dazzle of her smile.

"Miss Temple is an exceedingly charming woman," he said, when Mrs. Elbridge had quitted the room. "She and Miss Bodney were schoolmates, I believe."

THE FAMILY JOKE.   27

"Yes, and although much separated, have not broken the gauze bonds of school fellowship."

"Gauze bonds, Judge?"

"The beautiful but flimsy friendship of girlhood."

"Younger than Miss Bodney, I fancy."

"Yes, a year or so. She lives in Quincy, and is here for a month, but we shall keep her longer if we can. She is a source of great entertainment. Of course, you have noticed Florence closely—you couldn't help it. She is one of the sweetest creatures that ever lived, and she has character, too. I couldn't think more of her if she were my daughter —and she is to be my daughter. She and my son Howard are soon to be married. It is the prettiest romance in life or fiction. They are near the same age. They went to school hand in hand—sat beside each other at table, year after year, and in innocent love kissed each other good-night. They don't know the time when they made their first vows— upon this life they opened their eyes in love; an infant devotion reached forth its dimpled hand and drew their hearts together. Beautiful."

The preacher was thoughtful for a few moments, and then he said: "The Spirit of God doing the work it loves the best. And they are soon to be married. May I hope to—"

"You shall join them together, Bradley."

"I thank you."

"No, thank the memory of your father. I knew him well. He was my friend at a time when friendship meant something to me."

"And the young woman's brother, Judge. I haven't seen much of him."

"George Bodney? A manly young fellow, sir, quiet and thoughtful. He and Howard are to take up the law when I put it down—indeed, they have begun already."

"You are a happy man, Judge."

The Judge leaned back in his chair and was thoughtful; his cigar had gone out, and he held it listlessly. "Yes, for the others are so happy." He dropped the cigar stub upon the ash tray, roused himself, and said: "Nothing bothers me now. I am out of the current of life; I am in a quiet pool, in the shade; and I don't regret having passed out of the swift stream where the sun was blazing. No, I am rarely worried. Yes, I am annoyed at times, to be perfectly frank, now, for instance, and by a most peculiar thing. I—er—a friend of mine told me a story that bothers me, although it is but a trifle and shouldn't worry me at all. He is a lawyer, situated very much as I am. He has been missing money from his safe. No one but himself knows the combination. He couldn't suspect either of his sons; they didn't know the combination—not to be considered at all. He doesn't keep large sums on hand, of course; just enough to accommodate some of his old-fashioned clients who like to do business in the old-fashioned way. It bothered him, for he took it into his head that he himself was getting up at night and in his sleep taking the money from the safe and hiding it somewhere. For years, whenever he has had anything important on hand, he has been in the habit of waking himself at morning with an alarm clock. And I told him to set the clock in the safe and catch himself. He has done better than that—has fixed a gong so that it will ring whenever the inner drawer of the safe is pulled open. Of course, it is nothing to me, but—ah, come in, Agnes."

"Your wife has sent a bench warrant for you," said the young woman, entering the room and shaking her finger at the Judge.

"To be served by a charming deputy," said Bradley.

She laughed. "No wonder preachers catch women," she replied. "I'm glad I struck you. I was afraid I might miss."

The Judge arose and bowed to her. "We might dodge an arrow but not a perfume," said he.

"Now, Mr. Judge, when did you come from the South?" she cried. "But are you going with me? There are some more people in there; a young fellow that looks like a scared rabbit. But he's got nerve enough to say cawn't. I told him that if he'd come to Quincy we'd make him say kain't."

"Well, Bradley," said the Judge, "we are prisoners. Come on."

Bradley halted a moment to speak to Agnes. The Judge turned and asked if Howard and George Bodney were in the drawing room. She replied that Howard had gone or was going to a reception and that Mr. Bodney was somewhere about the house. She had seen him passing along the hall with Mr. Goyle. Just then, in evening dress, Howard came into the room. "I thought I heard Florence in here," said he, looking about.

"Going to leave us?" said the Judge.

"Yes, to bore and be politely bored. I want Florence to see if I look all right."

"Oh, I wonder," cried Agnes, "if any man will ever have that much confidence in me. There she is now. Florence, here's a man that wants you to put the stamp of approval upon his appearance."

Howard turned to Florence. "I wanted you to see me," he said.

"I've been looking for you," she replied.

Bradley, in an undertone, spoke to the Judge. "I can see the picture you drew of them."

"No," replied the preacher, with the light of admiration in his honest eyes.

Agnes spoke to Howard. "It must have been nearly half an hour since you and Florence saw each other. What an age," she added, with the caricature of a sigh. "But come on, Judge, you and Mr. Bradley." She led the two men away, looking back with another mock sigh at Florence.

"I may not be back till late," said Howard, "and I couldn't go without my good-night kiss."

She smiled upon him. "I knew that you had not forgotten it. And yet," she added, looking at him—"and yet I was anxious."

"Anxious?"

"Yes, but I didn't know why. Howard, within the past few days my love for you has taken so—so trembling a turn. We have been so happy, and—"

"And what, Florence?"

"Oh, I don't know, but something makes me afraid now. You know that there are times when happiness halts to shudder."

He put his arm about her. "Yes, we are sometimes afraid that something may happen because it has not. But it is only a reproachful fancy. We see the sorrow of others and are afraid that we don't deserve to be happy. But I must go," he added kissing her.

She continued to cling to him. "Do I look all right?" he asked.

"I don't know—I can't see."

"Can't see?"

"No. Love, which they say is blind, has blinded me."

He kissed her again. "But if love blinds, Florence, it would make a bat of me. You are serious tonight," he added, looking into her eyes.

"Yes, I am." The sound of laughter came from the drawing room. "Yes, I am, and I must go in there to be pleased. Howard, do you believe that anything could separate us?"

"Really, you are beginning to distress me. I have never known what it was to live without you, and I couldn't know it. But cheer up, won't you? To-morrow we—"

"Yes, I will," she broke in. "It was only a shadow and it has passed. But I wonder where such shadows come from. Why do they come? Who has the ordering of them?"

As they were walking toward the door opening into the hall, William entered from the passage, smoking his pipe, his thin hair rumpled as if he had just emerged from a contest. Howard and Florence did not see him, and he called to them.

"I say, there, Howard, I thought you were going out."

The young man halted and looked back with a smile. "Don't you see me going out, Uncle Billy?"

"Now look here, young fellow!" exclaimed the old man in a rage, his hair seeming to stand up straighter, "I don't want to be Uucle Billied by you, and I won't have it, either. Your daddy's got it in for me lately, and I'll be hanged if I'm going to put up with it much longer. And Florence, you'd better speak to him about it. I want to give him every opportunity to mend his ways toward me, and you'd better caution him before it's too late. Do you understand?"

"Yes, Uncle William," she answered. "And I will speak to him."

"Well, see that you do. And, mind you, I wasn't certain whether it was on the tenth or the eleventh;

I was willing to give either the benefit of the doubt; I—"

"That's all right, Uncle William," said Howard.

The old man glared at him. "It's not all right, sir, and you know it. But go ahead. I don't belong to the plot of this household, anyway. I'm only a side issue." Howard and Florence passed out, and he shouted after them. "Do you hear me? Only a side issue."

Just then Bodney came in. "You are a what, Uncle William?" he asked, looking about.

"I said a side issue."

"What's that?"

"If you haven't got sense enough to know, I haven't the indulgence to tell you."

"Where did you get that pipe, Uncle William?"

"I got it in the Rocky Mountains," said the old fellow.

"It must have come there about the time the mountains arrived. Whew!"

"Now, look here, George Bodney, don't you bring up the tail end of an entire evening of insult by whewing at my pipe. I won't stand it, do you hear?"

Bodney undoubtedly heard, but he did not reply; he went over to the desk and began to look about, moving papers, as if searching for something. "I left my knife here, somewhere," said he. "Must have a little more light." He turned up the gas drop light on the table, went back to the desk, and, pretending to find his knife, turned down the drop light lower than it had been before.

"There's no use to put out the light simply because you've found your knife," said William. "It may be to your advantage to have it dark, but I like to see. I haven't always lived in this soot and smoke; I have lived where I could see the sky from one year's end to another."

"I beg your pardon," said Bodney, "but how long do you expect to stay in this room?"

"Oh, don't pay any attention to me. I don't belong to the plot."

"What plot?" Bodney exclaimed, with a start.

"Why, the plot of this household—the general plot of the whole thing."

"Oh, yes, I see," said Bodney.

"I'm glad you do. And, here, just a minute. The Judge and I had a difference tonight."

"Not a serious one, I hope."

"Devilish serious. Wait a moment. I set out by admitting that I was not exactly certain whether it was on the tenth or the eleventh. But I settled it, finally, I think, on the eleventh. I—"

"Eleventh of what?"

"Of June, sixty-three. On that day, as I started to tell them—now, I want to be exact, and I'll tell you all about it." The old man sat down, crossed his legs, took a few puffs at his pipe, preliminaries to a long recital; but the young fellow, standing near, began to shift about in impatience. "I remember exactly what sort of a day it was. There had been a threat of rain, but the clouds—"

"Oh, I don't care anything about it."

"What!"

"I say, I don't care anything about it."

"The hell you don't! Why, you trifling rascal, I raised you; you owe almost your very existence to me. And now you tell me that you don't care anything about it. Go on out, then. You shan't hear it now, after your ingratitude." Bodney strode out, and the old man shouted after him, "I wouldn't tell you that story to save your life." Laughter came from the drawing room. William grunted contemptuously. "There's John telling his yarns. And that preacher—why, if I couldn't tell a better story than a preacher—" He broke off and got up with sudden energy. "But they've got to hear that story. They can't get away from it." And muttering, he walked out briskly.

Bodney stepped back into the room. He looked at the light, turned it lower, sat down and, leaning forward, covered his face with his hands. But he did not remain long in this position; he got up and went to the safe, put his hand upon it, snatched it away, put it back and stood there, gazing at the light. Then he went to the door and beckoned. Goyle, disguised as Howard, walked in with insolent coolness. In Bodney's room he had dressed himself, posing before the glass, arranging his bronze beard, clipping here and there, touching up his features with paint—and Bodney had stood by, dumb with astonishment. The dress suit, everything, was complete, and when he came out he imitated Howard's walk. Bodney could not help admiring the superb control he had of his nerves; but more than once he felt an impulse to kill him, particularly when, in response to the beckoning, he stepped into the office.

"If it fails, I shoot you," Bodney whispered.

"Rot. It can't fail. Don't I look like him?"

"Yes. You would deceive me—you—"

"Art, bold art," said Goyle. "A man ought to be willing to die for his art. Turn the light a little higher."

"No, it's high enough."

Goyle walked over leisurely and turned up the light. "That's better. We must give him a chance to see."

"Wait a moment," said Bodney, as Goyle took his position at the safe. "Wolf, I want to acknowledge myself the blackest scoundrel on the earth."

"Not necessary. Taken for granted. Go ahead."

Bodney turned to go, but hesitated at the hall door and seemed again to struggle with something that had him in its grasp. Goyle motioned, and said, "Go ahead, fool." Bodney passed into the hall, and Goyle began to turn the knob of the safe, holding his paper to catch the light. He heard the voice of Bodney. "It won't take long. I want you to help me—" The door swung. Goyle pulled open the drawer, and then followed three sharp strokes of the gong, just as loud laughter burst from the drawing room. Goyle jumped back. The Judge rushed in, with Bodney clinging to him. Goyle turned as if he had not seen the Judge and rushed from the room. Bodney struggled with the Judge, his hand over his mouth, and forced him down upon a chair. "Judge, father, not a word—for his mother's sake. You must freeze your heart for her sake." The old man dropped with a groan, Bodney bending over him.

Goyle began to turn the knob of the safe.

CHAPTER III.

THE NIGHT CAME BACK WITH A RUSH.

Bodney led the Judge to his room on the second floor, where he left him almost in a state of collapse. He spoke of calling Mrs. Elbridge, but the old man shook his head, which Bodney knew he would do, and in a broken voice said that he wanted to be left alone. At the time when the Judge left the drawing room with Bodney, Bradley was bidding the family good-night, but lingered a moment longer to join the company in a laugh at William, who, having settled his date to his own satisfaction, had forgotten the point of the story.

Bodney's room was on the first floor, off the passage, and, going thither, he found Goyle sitting on the side of the bed, not as Howard, but as himself. The scoundrel declared that it had worked like a charm, but that the clang of the gong had prevented his getting any money. That, however, was a minor consideration. He needed money, it was true; he had not expected much, but even a little would have helped him greatly. A lower order of mind might have brooded over the disappointment, but his mind was exultant over the success of his art. He argued that if his impersonation of a son could deceive a father, he might bring forth a Hamlet to charm an audience.

"How is he?" Goyle asked, as Bodney stepped into the room.

"Don't talk to me, now," said Bodney, sitting down. He took up a newspaper and fanned himself. "For a time I wished that I had killed you."

"Yes? And now?"

"I wish that you had killed me. Tell me, are you a human being? I don't believe you are. I don't believe that any human being could have the influence over me that you have had—that you still have, you scoundrel. I wish I could stab you."

"Can't you?"

"No. My arm would fall, paralyzed. I used to scout the idea of a personal devil, but I believe in one now. He is sitting on my bed. He has compelled me to do something—"

"It worked like a charm, George; and now, old fellow, don't hold a grudge against me. I have taught you more than you ever learned before; I have shown you that a man can do almost anything—that men are but children to be deluded by trickery. There, for instance, is a judge, a man who was set up to pass upon the actions of men. What did I do? Convinced him that his own son is a robber. Was that right? Perhaps. Why should such a man have been a judge? What wrongs may not his shortsightedness have caused him to commit? We can't tell. He may have committed a thousand unconscious crimes. But an unconscious crime may be just as bad as a conscious one. He has been sitting above other men. Now let him suffer; it is due him. And his son! What does he care for you or me? He reads, and thinks that he is wise. He has stuffed himself with the echo of feeble minds; and now let him wallow in his wisdom. Look at me. Are you sorry for what we have done? Look at me."

Bodney made an effort to get up, but his strength seemed to fail him, and he remained as he was, gazing at Goyle. "George," Goyle continued, his eyes glittering, "I was the hope of a father, a better man than Judge Elbridge. But he was ruined by honest men and died of a broken heart. That was all right; it was a part of life's infamous plan. Everything is all right—a part of the plan. My friends called me a genius; they believed that I was to astonish the world, and I believed it. I bent myself to study, but one day the bubble burst and I felt then that nothing amounted to anything—that all was a fraud. The world is the enemy of every man. Every man is the natural enemy of every other man. Evil has always triumphed and always will. The churches meet to reform their creeds. After a while they must revise out God—another bubble, constantly bursting. Then, why should there be a conscience? That's the point I want to make. Why should you and I suffer on account of anything we have done? Everything you see will soon pass away. Nothing is the only thing eternal. Then, let us make the most of our opportunities for animal enjoyment. The animal is the only substance. Intellectuality is a shadow. Are you sorry for what I have done?"

He fixed his glittering eyes upon Bodney, and, gazing at him, Bodney answered: "No, I am not. It was marked out for us, and I don't suppose we could help it; but somehow—somehow, I wish that I had killed you."

"What for? to cut off a few days of animalism—to make of me an eternal nothing? That wouldn't have done any good."

"It would have prevented the misery—"

Goyle stopped him with a snap of his fingers. "For how long? For a minute. It will all pass away. Be cheerful, now. We haven't any money as a reward of our enterprise and art, but we have let the life blood out of all suspicion attaching to us. Let us go to bed."

"You go to bed. I will lie on the floor."

"No use to put yourself out, George. I'll lie on the floor."

"No," said Bodney, and Goyle let him have his way. The hours passed, Bodney lying in a restless stupor, but Goyle slept. Sunlight poured into the room and Bodney got up. He went to the window and stood to cool his face in the fresh air. He looked back at the bed. Goyle was still sleeping, breathing gently. The horror of the night came in a rush. And there was the cause of it, sleeping in peace. Bodney snatched open a drawer and seized a razor. Goyle turned over, with his face toward the window.

"Ah, up? What time is it, George?"

Bodney dropped the razor and sat down. "It is time to get up," he said. Goyle got out of bed and began to exercise himself by striking out with his fists. He had passed, he said, a night of delicious rest, with not a dream to disturb him. He whistled merrily as he dressed himself. Bodney stood with his elbow resting on the marble top of the "bureau," his face yellow and haggard. Glancing down into the half closed drawer, he saw the razor and shuddered at the sight of it. With his left hand he felt of his right arm, gripping it from shoulder down to wrist as if in some strange manner it had been deprived of strength. Goyle moved toward him and he pushed against the drawer to close it, but the keen eye of the "artist" fell upon the open razor, and glittered like the eye of a snake. But he showed no sign of fear or even of resentment.

"I will stay to breakfast with you," he said, putting his hand on Bodney's shoulder.

"I wish you wouldn't," Bodney feebly replied.

"Oh, no you don't. Come, brace up now. My part of the work is done, but yours is just beginning. I have saved you from suspicion, but you must keep yourself saved. That's right, brighten up. Now you are beginning to look like yourself. Why, nothing so very bad has been done. We have enacted a little drama, that's all. Such things, or things on a par with them, are enacted every day. The newspapers are full of stranger things. We haven't hired a 'castle' and entered upon a career of wholesale murder; we haven't cut up a woman and made her into sausage."

The voice of William was heard in the passage, scolding a housemaid for disturbing his papers. The old man tapped on the door and Goyle opened it.

"Ah, you here?" said the old man, stepping into the room. "You'd better go in to breakfast. Well, sir, I never saw anything like it in my life. I can't put a thing down and find it where I left it. George, what's the matter with you this morning?"

"Nothing at all, sir. I had a headache and didn't sleep very well. That's all. Is the Judge up yet?"

"I believe not. And when he does get up I want to have a talk with him. I'll be hanged if he didn't get that preacher to laughing at me last night— laughing at me right here in my own house. I can stand a good deal, but when a preacher laughs at me, why things have gone too far."

Goyle smiled upon him. "But, Mr. Elbridge, a preacher means quite as little when he laughs as when he talks."

This pleased the old man, and he chuckled, his fat sides shaking. Bodney smiled, too, and Goyle gave him a look of approval and it appeared to brighten him. He dressed himself hastily, turning occasionally to heed a remark made by Goyle or the old man, and when he stepped out of the room to go with them to breakfast, his face was not so yellow, nor his countenance so haggard.

CHAPTER IV.

STOOD LOOKING AT THEM.

About two hours later Florence was sitting alone in the drawing room when Howard entered. She asked him if he had seen his father that morning. He sat down on a sofa beside her and said, after a moment's reflection:

"Yes, I have seen him? Why did you ask?"

She seemed worried and did not immediately answer him. He repeated his question. "Because he spoke of you at breakfast," she said. "He didn't appear at all well—sat staring about, and—"

"That explains it," said Howard.

"Explains what?" she asked.

"His treatment of me."

"Treatment of you? Has anything gone wrong?"

"Yes, in the office, just now. When I went in he jumped up from his desk, threw down a hand full of papers, and stared at me—muttered, seemed to struggle with himself, sat down, and asked me to leave him alone. He never acted that way toward me before. I'm afraid he's ill. Why, he's the most jovial man in the world, and—I'm worried. I don't understand it. If he's sick, why didn't he say so?"

"I don't know, but don't let it worry you, dear," she said.

"But it does, Florence, to be turned upon in that way. What did he say about me at the table this morning? He surely wasn't angry because I didn't get up in time for breakfast."

"Surely not. He didn't say anything, only asked where you were, and kept staring at the place where you sit."

"And is that the reason you asked me if I had seen him?"

"Yes, that and the fact that he didn't appear to be well."

"I don't understand it. Why, he has joked with me all my life, sick or well. It hurts me." And, after a slight pause, he added: "I wonder if he turned on George, too."

"It wouldn't seem so, for as he was going out of the breakfast room he put his hand on brother's shoulder and leaned on him."

Bodney came in at that moment, and, looking about, asked if they had seen Goyle. As he was going out, Howard called him.

"Oh, George, just a moment. Have you noticed anything strange about father this morning?"

And Bodney was master of himself when he answered: "Nothing much. Only he didn't seem to be as well as usual. It will pass off. I wonder where that fellow is?" He strode out, and they heard him talking to Goyle in the hall.

"Put his hand on George's shoulder and leaned on him," Howard mused, aloud. "Then he is not well. George knows it and doesn't want to distress me by telling me. Did he sit up late?"

"No. Mr. Bradley had to go early, and just as he was taking his leave brother stepped in and asked your father to help him with an important matter—some abstract of title, or something of the sort, and they went out and he didn't come back. I don't want to distress you, but your mother said that he walked the floor nearly all night."

"Did she? And George knows more than he is willing to tell. But why do they try to shield me? It would be all right to shield mother if anything were wrong, but if there's a burden, I ought to help bear it."

She besought him not to be worried, assuring him that nothing had gone very far wrong and that everything would come right. The clearness and the strength of her mind, her individuality, her strength of character, always had a quick influence upon him, and he threw off the heavier part of his worry and they talked of other matters, of the reception which he had attended the night before. He repeated a part of a stupid address delivered by a prominent man, and they laughed at it, he declaring that nearly all men, no matter how prominent or bright, were usually dull at a reception. And, after a time, she asked: "What sort of a man is Mr. Goyle?"

"Oh, he's all right, I suppose; smart, full of odd conceits. I don't know him very well. He comes into the down-town office quite frequently, but he rarely has much to say to me. George seems to be devoted to him."

Florence shook her head, deploring the intimacy. "I don't like him," she said. "And Agnes says she hates him. She snaps him up every time he speaks to her." She looked at Howard, and saw that his worry was returning upon him. She put the hair back from his forehead, affection's most instinctive by-play, and said that he must not be downcast at a mere nothing, a passing whim on the part of his father. "And it was only a whim," she added.

"But whims make an atmosphere," he replied.

"Not ours, Howard—not yours, not mine. Love makes our atmosphere."

"Yes," he said, putting his arm about her, "our breath of life. Florence, last night you were depressed, and now I am heavy." Their heads, bent forward, touched each other. "And your love is dearer to me now than ever before." Their faces were turned from the hall door. The Judge silently entered, and, seeing them, started toward them, making motions with his hands as if he would tear them apart. But Howard, after a brief pause, spoke again, and the old man halted, gazing at them. "Florence, you asked me, last night, if anything could separate us, and now I ask you that same question. Could anything part us?"

"No," she said, "not man, not woman, nothing but God, and he has bound us together."

"With silken cords woven in the loom of eternity," he replied; and the Judge wheeled about, and, with a sob, was gone, unseen.

"What was that?" Florence asked, looking round. "It sounded like a sob."

"We were not listening for sobs and should not have heard them," he replied. "It wasn't anything."

William came in, clearing his throat. "Don't let

me disturb you," he said, as they got up. "I don't belong to the plot at all." He began to look about. "I left my pipe somewhere."

"I don't think it's here, Uncle William," said Howard. "You surely wouldn't leave it here; and, besides, I don't hear it."

There came a sort of explosion, and upon it was borne the words, "What's that? You don't hear it? You don't? Now what have I ever done to you to deserve such an insult? Ha! What have I done?"

"Why, nothing at all, Uncle William."

"Then why do you want to insult me? Haven't I been your slave ever since I came here? Haven't I passed sleepless nights devising things for your good? You can't deny it, and yet, at the first opportunity, you turn upon me with an insult."

"Why, Uncle Billy," said Florence, "he wouldn't insult you. He was only joking."

Howard assured him that he meant no insult, whereupon the old man said: "All right, but I know a joke as well as anybody. I have joked with some of the best of 'em in my time, I'll tell you that. But it's no joke when you come talking about not hearing a man's pipe. It's a reflection on his cleanliness—it means that his pipe is stronger than a gentleman's pipe ought to be. But I want to tell you, sir, that it isn't. It's as sweet as a pie."

Howard said that he knew the import of such an accusation. "But," he added, "I was in hopes that it was strong, not to cast any reflection, you understand, but to show my appreciation of what you have done for me. I was going to give you that meerschaum of mine."

The old man's under jaw dropped. "Hah? Well, now, I do believe that it has got to be just a little nippy; just a little, you understand."

"I wish it were stronger than that, Uncle Billy."

"You do? Howard, you have always been a good friend to me; our relations have been most cordial and confidential, and I don't mind telling you—to go no further, mind you—that my old pipe is as strong as—as a red fox. Yes, sir, it's a positive fact. Er—where is your pipe?"

"In my room. You may go and get it as soon as you like."

"All right, and I'm a thousand times obliged to you. Florence, did that preacher go away so suddenly last night because I settled the fact that it was on the tenth?"

"Oh, no, he left because he had an engagement."

"Well," drawled the old man, "I don't know

about that. Why, confound him, I've got a right to settle it as my memory dictates. Does he think that I'm going to warp my recollection just for him?"

"What was it all about, Uncle Billy?" Howard asked.

"About a story I was going to tell."

"Did you tell it?"

"Did I tell it! Well, after a fashion; after they had badgered me. Then I made a mess of it. How do you expect me to tell a story when—look here, ain't you trying to put it on me? Hah, ain't you?"

"I don't know what you mean, Uncle William."

"Oh, you don't. The whole kit of you are devilish dull all at once."

"You surely don't include me," said Florence.

"No, not you, Florence, but all the men about the house. Why, I went up to John, just a while ago, and I'll be hanged if he didn't snap at me like a turtle—told me to get out of his office. Shall I tell you what he said? He said that last night he went to hell and was still there. There's something wrong with him, as sure as you live."

Howard turned away and began to walk up and down the room. "There it is again," said he. "I no sooner convince myself that it might have been a mere whim when something comes up to assure me that it is something worse. And the look he gave me, Florence. It hurts me." He walked toward the door. Florence asked him if he were going to his father. He turned and stood for a moment in silence. "No, I am going down town. I don't feel right. I am hurt. But don't say anything to him, please. I am going to wait and see what comes of it. And please don't say anything to mother." He took his leave, and Florence went to the window and looked after him as he passed down the street. She spoke to William. "I wonder what the trouble is," she said.

"I don't know," William replied, ruffling his brow, "but as for that preacher—the first thing he knows, I won't let him come here. John has insisted on his dropping in at any time, because he used to know his father, but I'll attend to that. Why does a great, strong fellow as he is want to throw away his time? Why doesn't he get to work?" He sat down and, looking toward the piano, asked Florence to play something. "I'd like a tune quick and high-stepping," he said. She told him that she was in no humor. "In that event," he insisted, "you might play the Maiden's Prayer."

"Not now, Uncle William. Here's Agnes. She'll play for you."

"No, I won't," said Agnes, coming into the room. Florence expected the old fellow to snort his displeasure at so flat a refusal, but he did not. He bowed to her and said: "Now, that's the way to talk. I like to have a woman come right out and say what she means. Well," he added, getting up, "I am not in your plot, anyway, so I'll bid you good morning."

As soon as William was gone, Agnes went to the piano, seated herself on the stool and began to ripple on the keys. "There are times when we feel like dabbling in water but don't want to swim," she said.

"And you are dabbling now," Florence spoke up.

"Only dabbling. Oh, I forgot; your dressmaker is out there, and I came in to tell you."

"I'm glad you didn't forget it entirely. Oh, and I must tell you something. Brother says that Mr. Goyle is smitten with you."

Agnes, still rippling, turned half way round, sniffed and turned back. "I hate him so hard that it's almost second cousin to love," she declared.

"Don't let it be any closer kin, Agnes. There is always danger in a first cousin."

Agnes, still rippling, sniffed contemptuously.

"He's been following me around all the morning. How I love to hate him."

The voice of Mrs. Elbridge was heard, calling Florence, who answered that she was coming, but she halted long enough to say to Agnes, mischievously, that she might learn to love him if she loved to hate him. Both love and hate were kindred passions, with but a thin partition between them. As she was going out, Agnes shouted after her that, if she ever loved him she would hate herself, and then, just as Goyle and Bodney entered the room, she added: "We tar and feather such fellows in Quincy."

"You do what in Quincy?" Bodney asked.

And Agnes, without looking round, repeated: "Tar and feather such fellows."

Goyle knew that she meant him, but instead of kindling resentment, her words aroused in him an additional interest in her. He looked at her as in the rythmic sway of her graceful form, the nodding of her shapely head, she kept time with a tune, half remembered, half improvised; and, turning to Bodney, he asked in tones too low for the girl to hear: "Has she got any money?"

"I think she has."

"Leave me alone with her."

"Do you want to snatch her purse?"

"Do you suppose I want a hair pin, a pearl button, a scrap of verse, and a three-cornered piece of silk that no man can match? I mean, has she got any money in her own name?"

"I haven't asked her, but I think she has."

"Then leave me alone with her."

Bodney stood looking at him. There was a continuous fascination in the fellow's affrontery. "All right," he said, but quickly added: "We've got to go down town, you know. I'll step into the office and wait till she gets through with you. You may hypnotize me, but—"

Goyle cut him off with a gesture. "Nonsense! When she gets through with me! Cool, coming from a man whose honor I have saved at the risk of my own. But no cooler than the bullet you threatened me with."

"I wish I had given it to you," said Bodney.

"Do you? It's not too late, if you are bent on murder. But that's all right," he broke off, with a wave of the hand. "Leave me alone with her."

Bodney went out and Goyle sat down on a sofa, gazed at the girl, cleared his throat, coughed; but she did not look round. "What are you playing? May I ask?"

"You have asked," she replied, without looking round.

"But you haven't told me."

She left off playing, and slowly turned on the stool to face him. "A tune they played in Quincy one night, when they tarred and feathered a man," she said. And then, with a smile of sweet innocence, she added: "You were never in Quincy, were you?"

"Well, I was never tarred and feathered there."

"Possibly an acknowledgment that you were never in the town. Oh, somebody told me that you were once connected with opera."

"Then somebody flattered me. I couldn't sing in a chorus of scissors grinders."

"A sort of Chinese opera, I inferred," she said.

"Well, that's about the only sort I could sing in. Chinese opera, eh?"

"Yes, that's what I inferred. It was something about Sing-Sing. Isn't that Chinese?"

"Oh, it sounds like a joke," said he.

"And it wasn't?" she asked, in surprise. "Then it was serious opera instead of comic. They call serious opera grand, I believe. And is that the reason they call larceny grand—because it is serious?"

For a time he sat in a deep study of her. How

different from the nervous and impressionable weakling who had just left the room; and in looking at her he felt that his eyes refused to glitter with a snake-like charm; they were dull and flat, and he drew his hand across them. "Do you know that I like you?" he said.

"Then I do not bring up an unpleasant recollection."

"No, a beautiful vision." And now he had more confidence in his eyes, for he got up and moved toward her. She slipped off the stool and stood looking at him.

"Won't you play something for me?" he asked.

"I don't want to play. I don't feel like it."

"Let your fingers dream over the keys."

"My hands aren't asleep." She moved off from him.

"You aren't afraid of me, are you?"

She looked him in the eye. "My grandmother killed a panther," she said.

He drew his hand across his eyes; he recalled what Bodney had said—about her getting through with him. In the dictionary of slang there is a word to fit him: the resources of his "gall" were boundless. "Why don't you like me?" he asked. "Am I ugly in your sight? Do I look like a villain?"

"If you looked more like a villain you'd be less dangerous."

"That's cruel. We may not see each other again. Won't you shake hands with me?"

"What is the use of shaking hands with a stranger we are never to see again," she said.

"But if we shake hands," he persisted, "we may not be strangers."

"No? Then, we'll not shake."

William strolled through the room, halting just long enough to assure them that he was not trying to break into the plot. "He's a queer duck," said Goyle.

"I wish there were more of his feather," she replied. "He can pass through without stopping."

"And so could I but for you," he rejoined.

She snapped her eyes at him. "What nerve tonic do you take?"

"Nature's. She gives me a tonic whenever I look at you."

She laughed at this, and she said: "I am woman enough to like that sort of talk, but I don't like you."

"You like my talk, but don't like me. Why this discrepancy? Why don't you like me?"

"Oh, I don't know. You give me the creeps."

"You are very frank."

"Oh, the creeps would make anybody frank."

Bodney appeared at the door and cleared his throat to attract attention, and he was bold enough to ask her if she had got through with him. "Long ago," she answered. "And now you may have him."

Goyle bowed to her. "Mr. Bodney and I may go out of town for a day or two—or, at least, I may. Will you permit me to hope to see you upon my return?"

"Oh, certainly," she said, and he felt that at last he was making some sort of progress. "I thank you," he replied.

But there was something more to follow. "You can hope that you may, and I will hope that you may not," she said.

Goyle bowed, and looked at her, admiringly. "Miss Needle-tongue," he said. "But you catch me."

Bodney told him to come on, but he lingered a moment longer. "May I tell you good-bye?" he said, and she replied that she hoped so. As the two men were going out the Judge came in. Goyle glanced at him, but Bodney averted his eyes. The old man's face smote him with reproach.

CHAPTER V.

SHE SAID THAT SHE WAS STRONG.

Agnes, accustomed to joke with the Judge, now looked at him in astonishment; his face was haggard and his eyes appeared hot with suffering. But he had not forgotten his dignified courtesy. He bowed to her, bade her good morning, as if he had not seen her earlier in the day, said that he was looking for Florence, and asked if she would please find her, that he desired to see her—alone. Agnes went out at once to find Florence, wondering what could have happened to throw so serious a cast upon the countenance of the Judge; and, left alone, the old man walked slowly up and down the room, talking to himself. "I don't know how to tell her, but she must know of it. It is my duty to tell her." He paused, looked toward the door, and continued: "I am striving to master my heart by smothering it; I must be the master of a dead heart." He paused again and resumed his walk. "Yesterday the world was a laugh, but today it is a groan. I wonder if he saw me. No, and toward him I must bear the burden of silence. A mother's heart would see the accusation in his face, and I must protect her. To keep her shielded is now my only duty in life. That decadent book! It was a seed of degeneracy. Ah, come in," he said, as Florence appeared at the door. Howard had called her eyes the searchlights of sympathy; and she turned those lights upon the old man's face as she came into the room, slowly approaching him.

"Did you send for me—father?"

"Father," he repeated with a catch in his breath that sounded like a sob. "My dear, it comes sweet from your lips, but it falls upon me with reproach." He stood with bowed head, and Florence put her hand on his arm.

"What is the matter, father? Why, you need a doctor. Let me call—"

"No!" came from him like a cry of pain, as he stepped back from her. "You must call no one. Wait a moment. Oh, I've got iron in me—but it is cold, Florence—cold. Wait a moment. Wait."

She stood looking at him, wondering, striving to catch some possible forecast of what might follow, but in his face there was no light save the dull hue of agony. Gradually he became calmer, and then he said: "I am going to tell you something; it is my duty."

"Yes, sir, I am listening."

"But are you strong enough to hear what I have to say?"

"Does it take strength to hear?"

"In your case—yes."

"Then I am strong." She moved closer and stood resolutely before him, looking into his eyes.

"Florence, I know your character; I know that your word is too sacred to break, but this is—is an unparalleled case, and you must be put under oath."

"Judge, instead of administering an oath, you ought to take medicine. Why, I never saw you this way before."

She was about to turn away from him, but he took her by the arm. "Look at me. You never saw me this way before. No. In all my experience I have never heard of a man being so situated. I am a novelty of distress. And you must know what my ailment is, but you must take an oath, a sacred oath, not to speak of it to any human being."

"But if it is so awful, why should I know it? Tell it to a physician."

"It is my duty to tell it to one human being, and you are the one."

"Then I will take the oath."

"Hold up your right hand." She obeyed him. "You swear never to repeat what I tell you."

"Yes, I swear."

"By the memory of your mother?"

"Yes, by the memory of my mother."

"And you hope that the Eternal God may frown upon you if you do not keep your oath?"

"Judge, this is awful."

"Are you going to back out now? Are you afraid?"

"I am not afraid. I hope that the Eternal God may frown upon me if I do not keep my oath."

He took her hand, the hand held high, and said to her, "You will keep your oath. It was disagreeable to take it, but the measure was necessary. And now comes the agonizing part of my duty—and I wish I had died before being compelled to discharge it. Florence, you know that I love you."

"Yes, sir, I know it—could never have doubted it. But why do you speak of it? What has it to do with—"

"Wait. This shall be explained. You must not marry my son."

She stepped back from him and from her clear

eyes, always so sympathetic, there came a flash of anger. "You are mad, Judge," she said.

"I grant it. He drove me mad—he sent me to hell."

"And you would drag me there."

"I would save you. It is a duty I owe to the memory of your father and to my own love for you. Yes, it is my duty."

"And it is my duty," she said, with now the light of sympathy in her eyes, "to send for a doctor."

"Wait. You have not heard. Remember you have sworn."

"Yes, and I will keep my oath. No, I have not heard. You have told me nothing. You have simply been mad enough to say that we must not marry." The sympathy had gone from her eyes. "You must know that Howard and I have all our lives lived for each other. I owe you nearly everything, I would make almost any sacrifice for you, but when you even intimate—but I will not reproach you," she said, softening again. "You have not told me why," she added, looking into his eyes.

"My child, it would break your heart."

She straightened and put her hand upon her bosom. "I offer my heart. Break it."

"Florence, my son Howard is a thief."

She snatched her hand from her bosom and raised it as if to strike him, but one look of agony from his eyes, and her hand fell. "Judge, how can you say such a thing? Something has tripped your mind, but how could it fall so low?"

"My mind has not been tripped. It is as firm as a rock. And you cannot doubt my word. Last night I saw him stealing money from the safe, as if I had not always supplied all his wants, and at an alarm which I had fixed, little dreaming who the thief might be, he ran away—a thief. You cannot doubt my word."

Stern of countenance and with her eyes piercing him, regal as the barbaric queens we find in ancient fiction, she stood, and the moment of her silence seemed an age to him. "I pity your word and I doubt your eyes."

"You may pretend to, but you cannot in your heart. You must believe me when I say that I saw him."

"You saw a vision. Your eyes have lied to you."

"I saw no vision. My eyes told a heart-breaking truth. Florence, would you marry a thief?"

"Sir, I would marry Howard if I knew that he had stolen a hammer to nail a god to the cross."

The old man wheeled away from her with a cry. "Oh, crumbled hope—"

Mrs. Elbridge swept into the room, gazing at the Judge. "Why, what is the matter?"

The old man gripped himself together. "Why, I—I have just received a dispatch, telling me—telling me that my brother Henry is dead. Don't tell William—brother Henry is dead."

Mrs. Elbridge went to him and put her arm about him. "And you loved him so," she said. "Poor, dear man, but we must bow to it, and pray for consolation. Don't—don't grieve so, dear. Where is the message?"

The old man looked at Florence. "It distressed him so that I tore it to pieces and threw it away," she said.

The Judge gave her a grateful look. "I thank you," he muttered.

CHAPTER VI.

THE WEXTON CLUB.

When Goyle and Bodney left the house they went to a place known as the Wexton Club. This institution was not incorporated under the laws of the state, but its affairs were conducted under a law, the law that governs the game of poker. The public dinner pail gaming house, the pickpocket of the laborer, had been closed; the grave-countenanced faro dealer and the sad-eyed man who turned the roulette wheel; the hoarse-voiced "hazard" operator, and the nimble and enterprising thief of the "stud poker" game, now thrown out of visible employment, stood at the mouth of the alley waiting for "good times" to return. "Bucket-shops" broke out in new places, once in a while, and there was the occasional raid of a poolroom, but it was agreed that public gambling was a thing of the rough and disgraceful past. But the poker clubs! They were not traps set for the man in overalls. His pennies and dimes were not solicited. Of course, if he saved up capital to the amount of five dollars, and came with a reasonable appearance of respectability, he could get into the game, but he was not wanted. The board of trade men, the race horse man, the merchant, doctor, lawyer, and particularly the fool with money, furnished the life blood of the enterprise. Shrewd gamblers risked their money and pronounced the game "straight." And it was "straight." The "house" could not afford to permit any "crooked" work. Its success, the "rake off," depended upon its own fairness to everyone playing in the game. But the "sucker" does not need to be cheated to lose. His own impulses will sooner or later rob him of all the money he can borrow, beg or steal. The man who plays for recreation wants it, not after a long season of waiting for a good hand, but at once; and putting in his money he draws to "short" pairs or to every four straight or four flush. He may have an encouraging spurt; he may make a hardened player wince and swear under his breath or even above it, but in the end, and it comes on apace, he shoves it back, broke, and the old-timer rakes in the money. Within recent years several fine young fellows of good standing and of bright prospects have looked for diversion in poker and have found state's prison. The road to the penitentiary is paved with four flushes.

At the Wexton, Goyle had introduced Bodney as his friend, Mr. Ramage, and out of that familiarity which comes of constantly gazing into a man's countenance, in the effort to determine what he holds in his hand, they shortened his name to Ram. The young lawyer had played with friends, and had won, not because his friends were kind to him, but because they were as experimental in drawing cards as himself, and because they were possessed of equally as much curiosity. The "gentleman's game" is a trap door, and it is easy enough to fall from "Billy" and "George" and "Tom," down into a hell on earth. This is not a tirade against gambling, for the horrors of that vice have engaged the ablest of pens, but to give life in poker clubs as it really exists, the attractive with the distressful. Indeed, the distress is not seen in the club. The victim gets up with a jocular remark, and silently goes out, wishing that he were dead, and resolving deep within his disconsolate heart that he will never enter the place again. Then his heart lightens. He is saved. He has lost money that he could not afford to lose, the very bread of his family; but he will do so no more. He has strength of purpose, an object in life, a position to maintain. He is now grateful to himself for his own strength of will. The next morning he goes dull and heavy to his business. He shudders as he enumerates the amount of money that he has lost within the past few weeks; counts it all up, and then, with a sickening pang, recurs a forgotten sum, borrowed from a friend and not yet returned, though he had promised to "hand" it back the next day. The details of his business are wearisome. At noon he goes out. At the "Club" they serve a meal, better than he can get at a restaurant. He will go there, but not to play. He plays, to get even—will try it once more; and at evening he sends a message to his wife—"detained on important business." He has several checks, and one by one they melt away in the pot. He is broke. He wants more chips. He has money in the bank, he declares; but the man at the desk is sorry to inform him that it is a rule of the "house" not to take personal checks. He is angry, of course. He wants to know why a check which he offered earlier in the evening was accepted, and is told that the other check was different, that it was signed by a name better known than his. Then he tries to borrow from the men who have won his money; he knows them well, for he has played with them day after day. They have laughed at his jokes, when with the fool's luck he has drawn to "short" pairs and won. They have no money to lend—would really like to accommodate him, but have obligations to meet. And so he goes heavily down the stairs again, with murder in his heart. But his heart lightens after a time. He will never, so help him God, play again. But he does. Ah, it is less bad to be bitten by a mad dog.

Goyle was but an indifferent player. He well knew the value of a hand, but was too impatient to wait. But no despair fell upon him when he lost. He did not look forward to a time when circumstances or the force of his own resolution might set him beyond the temptations of the game, but to the time when luck might give him enough money to put him in the game. Bodney, however, was bound soul and body. He could hardly think of anything else. Dozing to sleep he saw aces and kings; asleep, he drew to flushes and straights. In his sleep he might win, but only in his sleep. His soul seemed to have been created for this one debasing passion. It was his first, for though impressionable, no enthusiasm had ever mastered him, and love had never set his heart aflame. But now he was an embodiment of raging poker, not for gain, but for the thrill, the drunkenness of playing. His bank account, never large, was gone. For himself and for Goyle he had taken small sums of money from the Judge's safe, and had lived in the terror of being confronted with the theft. And he actually believed that had the old man accused him or even strongly suspected him he would have killed himself. Suspicion was now averted, but at the cost of what infamy! He could face Howard; he could endure with a show of self-control the agonized countenance of the old man; but remorse gnawed him like a rat. It was not to be supposed that Florence would be enlightened as to the coolness which, of necessity, must fall between Howard and the Judge, but it could not be otherwise than a grief to her. He could look forward and see the wonder in her eyes, and then the sorrow that must come to her. It is one of the misfortunes of a weak man to have a strong conscience, a conscience with not enough of forecast to prevent a crime, but one which agonizes when a crime has been committed. His only solace was to play. Then his mind was chained to the game, the dealing of the cards, the scanning of his hand, to the thrill of winning, the dull oppression of losing. Upon entering the club he had been surprised to see so many old and venerable looking men sitting about the tables. One had been a prominent lawyer; another, a doctor, had turned from a fine practice to waste his substance and the remainder of his days. There was good humor, an occasional story of brightness and color, but upon the whole the place was sad, everyone seeming to recognize that he was a hopeless slave The scholar turned poker-player, thinks and talks poker. He forgets his grammer, and puts everything in the present tense. "How did you come out last night?" someone asks, and he answers, "I lose." Many of those men would not have gone to a "regular" gaming house; they would not have played faro or roulette, but the blight of poker fell upon them, to weaken them morally, to make them liars. Sometimes an old fellow, getting up broke, would turn moralist. One said to Bodney: "The chips you see on the table don't belong to anyone. You may go so far as to cash them and put the money into your pocket, but it isn't yours. You may spend it, but you will borrow or steal to make it good to the game." Among those daily associates engaged in the enterprise of "wolfing" one another there was a fine shade of courtesy. No one can be politer or more genial than a winner, and a loser is expected to shove over the pot which he has just lost, in case the winner cannot reach it. In return for this the loser is permitted to swear at his victor, but etiquette demands that it shall be done in a mumble, as if he were talking to himself. The winner can stand a great deal of abuse. In the game there were usually two or more players put in by the "house," cool fellows, educated to know the value of a hand or the advantage of a position. They were the "regulars," the others the militia. The dash and the fire of the militiaman sometimes overrode the regular, but there was no question as to the ultimate result. The regular knew when to put down a bad hand; he could be "bluffed" by the militiaman. But he could afford to wait; he was paid to sit there; it was his business. Bodney, however, could not wait. With him, impulsive hope was leaping from deal to deal, from card to card, from spot to spot.

When Goyle and Bodney arrived the members of this family of interchangeable robbery were ranged at a long table in the dining room, eating in hurried silence or talking about the game. Occasionally someone would venture an opinion of a race horse or a prize fighter, but for the most part the meal was solemn and dull. Laughter was not unknown, but it was short, like a bark. This does not mean that there was a want of fellowship in the club, but eating was looked upon as a necessary interruption.

"You are just in time," said the proprietor of the house, not a bad fellow, a business man, accommodating as far as he could be, yielding sometimes to the almost tearful importunity of a fool to the extent of lending him money never to be returned. "Sit down. Fine weather we're having."

"A champagne day," said Goyle, sitting down and spreading a napkin across his knees. "How's the game going?"

"Oh, fairly well. We've got a good run of customers. They know that they are perfectly safe here."

"What's become of that fellow they called Shad?" asked a man at the end of the table.

"Oh, that fellow from Kansas City? He's gone. I didn't want him. I think he'd snatch a card."

Bodney was silent. He could hear the rat gnawing at his conscience, and he yearned for the moral oblivion of the game. Leaving Goyle at the table, he arose, and walked up and down, then went into the room where the game was forming. He had but fifteen dollars, but with this amount he felt that he could win. He bought ten dollars worth of chips, musing upon the fact that he had a reserve fund of five dollars. The game was all jackpots, twenty-five cent ante, and three dollar limit, except when the pot was doubled, and then the limit was five dollars. While a man at his side was shuffling a deck of new cards, Bodney began to meditate upon the policy which he intended to pursue. He would not draw to a flush or straight except when there were several "stayers," for then the percentage would warrant the risk. He would not draw to a pair below kings, nor open on jacks next to the dealer. If the pot were opened and came around to him, even without a raise, he would not stay on a pair of queens. If he opened on one pair and was raised, he would lie down. He would not stand a raise under kings up. Goyle came in, bought twenty dollars worth of chips, and took a seat on the opposite side of the table; and the game proceeded, with seven players. Bodney opened on a pair of kings. All passed around to Goyle. He looked at his hand a moment, and said: "Only one in? Well, I've got to stay. Give me that one," he said to the dealer, meaning that he wanted one card. "Got two little pairs here, and I won't raise you unless I help." Bodney drew three cards and did not help his kings. He bet a white chip. "Now I'll go down and look," said Goyle. "Bet you three dollars," he added. Bodney was smoking. He puffed at his cigar. "I don't know about that," he said. "What do you want to raise me for?"

"Got to play my hand, haven't I?" Goyle replied.

Bodney put his cigar on the table and thought. "Well, you've got 'em or you haven't. I'll call you." He threw in three blue chips, and Goyle spread a flush. "Thought you said you had two little pairs," said Bodney, as Goyle raked in the pot.

"I hadn't looked at my hand very close."

"You knew what you had all the time. Stayed on a four flush with only one man in. Of course you can always make it against me."

The deal went round and round, and occasionally Bodney won a pot, once a large one, and now as he stacked up his chips he felt at peace with the world. He laughed and joked with a man whom he had never met before; he did not see how he could lose. He threw off the rigor of his resolution, and drew to a pair of sixes, caught the third, raised the opener three dollars, and won the pot against aces up. Then his senses floated in a limpid pool of delight. Goyle opened a pot. Bodney raised him, having kings up. "I've got to stay," said Goyle. "Give me one card." Godney drew one and made a king full. His heart leaped with joy. "What do you do?" he asked.

"Bet three dollars," said Goyle, putting in the

chips, and Bodney was almost smothered in exultation.

"I raise you three."

"Raise *you* three," said Goyle.

"Are you as strong as that?" Bodney remarked, striving to hide the delight that was shooting through him. "Well, I'll have to raise you three."

Goyle began to study. "Well, if you can beat a jack full, take the money." He put in his three dollars. "King full," said Bodney, and Goyle threw down his cards with an oath. "Of course you couldn't make that against anybody but me. It's what a man gets for not playing his hand before the draw. I ought to have raised you back. Had three jacks all the time. But I didn't want to beat you."

"Looked like it when you made that flush."

"That's ancient history."

Bodney did not reply. He was behind a bulwark of chips, and his heart beat high. He began to tell a story. The winners were interested; the losers did not hear it. In the midst of the story, just below the climax, he had a hand beaten for six dollars, and the story, thus broken, fell into silence.

"What was that story you were going to tell?"

"It didn't amount to anything," said Bodney, but not long afterward he won a ten dollar pot, found the fragments of the story, lying at the bottom of silence, and gave them voice. The winners laughed; the losers did not hear it.

A minute legitimately employed may seem an hour; an hour at a poker table may be but a minute.

Someone asked the time. Bodney looked at his watch, and said that it was five o'clock. He was nearly seventy dollars ahead, with the reserve fund still in his pocket, and was resolved to quit very soon. Just then Goyle emerged from a contest, broke. "Let me take ten," said he. Bodney hesitated a moment. "Say, I've got to pay for—"

"Oh, I'll give it to you tomorrow. Let me take ten."

He passed over the chips, but with a feeling of depression. "I may be broke pretty soon," said he. "And I can't let you have any more."

"Broke pretty soon! Why, you're even on your whole life. You got all my money."

"I haven't won as much from you as you have from me."

"That's all right. My day may come."

Bodney was determined to play no longer than dinner time. Then he would cash in. Goyle's stack grew to the amount of thirty dollars. Bodney was glad to see it grow; ten dollars of it belonged to him. He did not care for ten dollars; he had loaned Goyle ten times ten, and did not expect to recover the sum, but chips were different, and especially now that they fed his passion and dulled his conscience. Goyle got up. "Let me have that ten till tomorrow," said he, and Bodney did not say anything, but his spirits felt a sudden weight. He was pleased, however, when Goyle went out, for there were to be no more raids upon his stack. Dinner was announced. He motioned to an attendant upon the game, and his chips were taken over to the desk.

"Going to quit us?" a man asked.

"Yes. This is the first time I've won," he added, by way of apology.

"Have dinner before you go," said the proprietor, coming forward.

"I don't know that I've got the time."

"Just as well. You've got to eat anyway."

He went out to dinner, and was permitted to be vivacious. An old fellow, sitting on his right, remarked: "I'm glad to see you win." Others said that they were glad to see him win. It was surely a very genial company.

CHAPTER VII.

WENT OUT TO "DIG."

After dinner, when the game was reorganized, Bodney looked on for a few moments, still alive to the keen pleasure of winning; and just as he was about to go out, a thought struck him. What was the use of quitting now that he had luck? He had waited for it a long time, and now that it had arrived he was going to throw it away. He might just as well win a hundred and seventy as seventy. He could at least try ten dollars, and quit if he found that fortune was against him. There was one vacant seat and he took it. Ten dollars and not a cent more. That would leave sixty to the good, enough to play on for a long time. So he bought ten dollars worth of chips and was again forgetful of the Judge, of Howard, of Florence, of the world. After a few hands he picked up a straight, seven high. He raised the opener, who promptly raised him in return, giving him the other barrel, as the saying went. Bodney raised again. He was to get action on all the money in front of him. The dealer said "cards," and the opener, tapping the table with his cards, replied, "Help him."

"Don't you want any?" Bodney eagerly asked.

"Didn't hear me call for any, did you?"

"Well, I don't want any either," said Bodney, in faltering tones. A seven high straight looked weak against a pat hand.

"Turn 'em over, boys," said the man in the lookout chair.

Bodney tremulously spread his hand. "Only seven high."

"Just top you. Mine's eight high. You had me scared, and if you'd have more money and bet me after the draw I don't think I call."

That might have been true, but it offered no consolation to Bodney. "Just my luck," he said.

"When a man gets them sort of hands beaten he's got to lose his money," said the "look-out." "There's nothing to it." A man standing near was waiting for Bodney's seat. He shoved back and was about to get up, pursuant upon the resolution which he had formed when, it occurred to him, as it always does, that with ten more he could win back the ten just lost. It was simply an accident that the fellow held over him. He would try ten more. His luck was gone, but he expected every moment to see it return. He opened a pot on aces and tens. A fool stayed on deuces, caught his third, and slaughtered him. He bought ten more. His spirits were heavy and he sighed distressfully. It was not the loss of the money; it was the harassing sense of being beaten. He opened another pot on queens up. One of the regulars raised him. He began to reason. "He would raise it on two pairs smaller than queens up. I saw him raise just now on sevens up. I'll stand it." He put in his money and drew one card. The regular drew one. The prospect was not bright, still it was not so bad. He did not help. He bet a white chip; the regular raised him three dollars and he called. Then the regular had recourse to a joke, new to Bodney, but old to the game. "I have the waiter's delight," said he.

"The what?"

"The waiter's delight," and he spread a tray full.

At ten o'clock, Bodney's capital, including the reserve fund, amounted to twenty dollars. "You beat me every time," he said, to an offensive fellow who sat opposite. It was the stranger with whom he had laughed early in the game.

"That's what I'm here for."

"That's all right. I'll get you yet."

He won several pots, and then opened a double pot for five dollars. He had a king high flush, and he intended the heavy opening to operate as a reverse bluff, to argue a small hand. The offensive fellow stayed and drew one card. He made a small full and Bodney felt his heart stop beating. At eleven o'clock he had simply the five dollar reserve fund. And he saw it melt away—saw his last chip go in. He drew, having a show for the pot, and made jacks up. The opener had queens up. Heavy of heart, Bodney went down the stairs. He cursed himself for playing after dinner. "If I only had ten dollars I might win it all back," he mused. "They can't possibly beat me all the time. I played as good cards as anybody. I wonder where I can get ten dollars. Everybody that knows me has gone home by now. Let me see. I know a fellow over at that drug store. But I've forgotten his name. Wonder if he'd let me have ten. I'll try him." He went into the drug store, saw the man standing behind the counter, walked up, reached over and shook hands with him.

"How's everything?" Bodney asked.

"Oh, pretty fair. How is it with you?"

"All right. Say, old man, a college chum of mine,

devilish good fellow, came in just now on a train and happened to catch me at the office—"

"Yes?" said the druggist, looking at him.

"Yes, and the fact is, he got here broke and has called on me to help him out. He's a devilish good fellow, and I don't exactly know what to do. Every one I know has gone home, and—could you let me have ten till tomorrow? You can count on it then."

"Oh, I guess so, but I'm rather short."

"I'll give it to you tomorrow without fail."

He went out with a ten dollar note crumpled in his hand. A man may fail to get rent money, clothes money, bread money; he may meet with obstacles that he cannot overcome; his self-respect withholds him from asking favors of certain men. But the fool in hot quest of poker money knows no self-respect, recognizes no embarrassments that might stand in modesty's way. Bodney bounded up the stairs, afraid that the game might have broken up. Panting and tremulous, he pressed the electric button. A negro porter pulled aside a blue curtain, peeped through the glass and opened the door. The game had not broken up. Every seat was taken, the regulars, with chips stacked high before them, the "suckers" squirming with "short money." How dull and spiritless everything had looked when Bodney went out, and now how bright it all was, the carpet, the window curtains, the pictures on the walls. The room was large, affording ample space for a meditative walk up and down, and as he was too nervous to sit still, he walked.

"Think there'll be a seat pretty soon?" he asked of the man at the desk.

"Very soon, I think. Sit down and make yourself comfortable. Have a cigar." He lighted the cigar and resumed his walk. Passing the table he saw a man in the death throes of a "show-down." Some one had opened a pot and he had been compelled to stay. Bodney eagerly watched the draw. The opener drew one card. The "show-down" man had to draw four, presumably to an ace. This was encouraging to Bodney. He was the next in line; he would get the seat. He leaned forward to catch the result. The opener had tens up. The four-card draw yielded a better crop, aces up, and with a sense of disappointment and injury Bodney resumed his walk. But pretty soon a man cashed in, and the young lawyer bought five dollars worth of chips, and took his seat. He won the first pot, the second and the third, but without stayers. Surely his luck had returned. Again he felt a current of pleasure flowing through his mind. He laughed at a stale joke. It had never sounded so well before. A man, the offensive fellow, now quite a gentleman, began to tell a story, and Bodney encouraged him with a smile. "I knew a man once, a preacher, by the way," said he, "who got into the habit of playing faro; I guess he must have played before he began to preach, and found that he couldn't quit. Some fellow that was kin to him croaked, and left him a lot of money. Then he knew he wouldn't play any more. Well, one day he went by the bank where he had his money, and pretty soon he says to himself: 'Believe I'll draw out just a small sum and try my luck once more—just once.' Well, he kept drawing on that money till it is all gone. Nothing to it, you know. Then one night he gets down on his knees and prays. 'Lord,' says he, 'if I ever play again I hope you'll make me lose.'"

"Did he play again?" Bodney asked.

"Yes; he keep right on."

"And did he lose?"

"No. He coppers his bets."

Bodney was immensely tickled at the idea of the fellow "coppering" his bets to offset the influence of the Deity, and he laughed uproariously, but just then he lost a pot, and his mirth fell dead. And after this every time he opened a pot someone would raise him. After a while he dragged out his last five dollars and invested in chips. Then he sank into the condition known as "sifting," anteing and never getting a pair. Behind him stood a man waiting for his seat. He saw his last chip melt away and he got up, so heavy that he could hardly stand. The fellow who had told the story, and to whom Bodney had paid the tribute of most generous laughter, dealt the cards and skipped Bodney without even looking at him. But Bodney looked at him, and how offensive he was. "I'd like to cut his infamous throat," he mused. Down the stairs again he went, heavier and more desperate than before. It was now past midnight. "Now what?" he said, halting on a corner and wiping his hot face. "I don't know what to do, but I almost know I could win out if I had ten more. But I don't know where to get it. There's no use to look for Goyle. I wonder if that fellow at the drug store would let me have another ten. I'll go and see." He crossed over, went into the drug store, and asked the squirter of soda water if his friend was there. No, he had gone home. "Is there anything I can do for you?"

"Well, I don't know. By the way, you've seen me in here a number of times, haven't you?"

"Oh, yes. And I used to see you over at the other place."

"Yes, I remember, now. And your name is—"

"Watkins."

"Yes, that's a fact. I remember you now. How are you getting along, Watkins?"

"All right."

"Yes, sir, I used to know you," said Bodney. "And I guess you are about the best in your line."

The man smiled. "Well, that's what they say."

"Yes, I've heard a good many people say it. Well, you understand your business. Say, can you do me a favor? I need ten dollars till tomorrow morning, and if you'll let me have it, I'll—"

The man shut him off with the shake of the head. "I haven't got ten cents," he said.

Bodney stepped out. "Come in again," the fellow called after him. He did not reply, except in a mumble, to hurl imprecations back over his shoulder at the soda-water man. "He's a liar, and I'll bet he's a thief. Now what?" he added, halting on the corner. He looked up and down the street, and scanned the faces of the passers-by, hoping to recognize an acquaintance. Presently a man rushed up and with a "helloa, old fellow," grasped him by the hand. Bodney gripped him; he did not recall his name, but he held him close. "I haven't seen you for some time," said Bodney.

"No, not since we were out on Lake Geneva, fishing for cisco."

"That's a fact. Say, everybody has closed up, and I need ten dollars till tomorrow morning. Can you—"

"I was just going to ask you for five," said the cisco fisherman. "I went over here at three sixty-one, and got into a little game of poker and got busted. Ever over there? Now, there's a good game, only two dollars limit, but it's liberal. There ain't a tight wad in the house. Come up some time."

Bodney got on a car to go home. He had just five cents. The talking of two women and the frolicking of a party of young fellows annoyed him. And then arose before him the sorrowful face of his sister. The rat had come back with his teeth sharpened, and he felt his heart bleeding. He fancied that he could hear the dripping of the blood. Then came upon him the resolve never to play another game of poker. It was a sure road to ruin, to despair. He would confess to Howard and the Judge. The car stopped and Bradley, the preacher, got on, sitting down opposite Bodney, who, upon recognizing him, arose and warmly shook his hand. "I am delighted to see you, Mr. Bradley. You are out thus late for the good of humanity, I suppose, or rather I know."

"I can only hope so," replied the preacher.

"Some sort of meeting of preachers for the advancement of morals, Mr. Bradley?"

"No, a dinner."

"Well, a good dinner contributes to good morals."

"If not over-indulged in."

"Yes, if there is a virtuous lack of wine, such as must have been the case tonight." He continued to stand, holding a strap, and meditating upon future procedure, for there was a purpose in the cordiality with which he had greeted the minister, a purpose now fully developed. "By the way, I must come down again tonight—am going home to get some money. Late this evening I received a note, telling me that a friend of mine, a divinity student, was exceedingly ill. I hastened to the number given and found him in a poverty-stricken room, lying upon a wretched bed, without a nurse, almost delirious with suffering. I knew that he was poor, that he had bent his energies to study to the neglect of material things, but I had not expected to find him in so deplorable a condition. So I am now on my way home to get ten dollars. I went to several places, hoping that I could borrow, but failed to find any one whom I knew well enough to ask for a loan, even for so short a time as tomorrow. But perhaps you could let me have it."

"Why, I'll go with you—at once. What is the young man's name?"

"Patterson. But he's so peculiar that he might not like to see a stranger. He begged me not to say anything about his condition."

Bradley gave him ten dollars, and he did not wait to reach the next street crossing, but jumped off the car, sprang upon a cable train going north, and was soon climbing the stairs leading to the Wexton Club. The same negro admitted him, and again he was afraid that the game might have dissolved, merely to cheat him of victorious reprisal, but it was still in progress, with one vacant seat. This time he invested his entire amount. The feeling of security, inspired by a reserve fund, favored an overconfidence, he fancied; it was better to know that there was nothing in reserve; it enforced caution. He played with varying luck till about twelve o'clock, till a regular smote him, hip and thigh; and then, like the captain, in the version of the poem, not recited to ladies, he staggered down the stairs.

CHAPTER VIII.

SAW THE BLACK FACE, GRIM, WITHOUT A SMILE.

It was nearly daylight when Bodney reached home. As he stood on the steps, after unlocking the door, he looked toward the east and said aloud: "The sun will soon draw to his flush. But he always makes it. God, what a night I've had. It is the last one, for here at the threshold of a new day I swear that I will never touch another card. And Goyle—I'll have nothing more to do with him." He went in, still repeating his vow, and as he passed the door of the office, was surprised to see a light within; and halting, he heard footsteps slowly pacing up and down. He stepped in and stood face to face with the Judge.

"Why, Judge, are you up so soon, or haven't you gone to bed?"

"I haven't been to bed. And you?"

"I have been sitting up with a sick friend. Don't you think you'd better lie down now?"

"No, I think nothing of the sort. It is better to

stand in hell, sir, than to wallow in it." Bodney sat down and the old man stood facing him. "But I can hardly realize that it was not a nightmare, George. Go over it with me; tell me about it. How did it happen?"

"Why, we simply came in here together and found—him. That's all."

"Yes, that's all, but it is enough."

"Was there very much money involved?" Bodney asked, not knowing what else to say.

"Money! I haven't once thought of the amount. It is the fact that I have been shot with an arrow taken from my own quiver, and poisoned. And yet, when I look at him, as I did today at dinner, I can hardly bring myself to believe my own eyes."

"You haven't—haven't said anything to him, have you?"

"In the way of accusation? No. It would leap from him to his mother. And I charge you to breathe it to no one."

"Not even my sister, who is to be his wife?"

"No. I will take her case in hand."

"But will you permit them to marry?"

"Not in a house of God; not in the presence of a guest. If she is determined to marry him against my protest, it must be in secret, as his deed was."

"I hope, sir, that everything may—may come out right."

"What do you mean by that?"

"Why, I hope that you may forgive him. I don't think that he's dishonest at heart."

"Then you are a fool."

"I admit that, Judge. I am a fool, an infamous fool."

"But you are not a scoundrel, not a thief."

"I might be worse."

"Enough of that. You are trying to debase yourself to raise him. Don't do it. You can't afford it. You have an honest living to make, and through you I must now look to the future." He turned away, and for a time walked up and down in silence; then, coming back, resumed his place in front of Bodney. "It all comes from my over-confidence in modern civilization. I did not presume to instruct or even advise him as to a course of reading, permitting him to exercise his own fancy; and it led him to that running sore on the face of the earth —Paris. He read French books, the germs thrown off by diseased minds. He lived in a literary pest house, and how could he come out clean? He was prepared for any enormity against nature, and why then should he have drawn the line between me and any of his desires?" He turned away, walking up and down, sometimes rubbing his hands together, as if washing them, then putting them behind him; halting at the desk to gaze down at something; going once to the safe and putting his hand upon it, but snatching it away as if the iron were hot. Bodney followed him about with his eyes, seeing him through cards, hearts and spades. His mind flew back to the game, and he could see the players sitting just as he had left them, the offensive fellow and the regular, behind a redoubt of chips. Only ten dollars more would have saved him; he had fancied so before, but now it was not fancy but almost a perfect knowledge. Why had he not asked the preacher for twenty instead of ten?

"But it is so strange," said the old man, sitting down with one arm straight out upon the green baize table; and the wretch with his mind on the game thought that it would be but an ungainly position for a player to take; he ought to sit facing the table with his hands in front of him. "Stranger than truth," said the Judge, and Bodney looked at him with a start. For a moment the game vanished and darkness fell upon the players, but soon a blue curtain was pulled aside, a black face, grim, without a smile, showed glistering behind the glass, the door was opened, and there again were the players in the light, the offensive fellow drawing one card, the regular solemn and confident with a hand that was pat. "Stranger than the strangest truth that I have ever encountered," the Judge went on, turning his back to the table and looking over Bodney's head at something on the wall. "But I brood too much."

"One card," said Bodney, in a thick muse.

"What's that?"

The young man started. "Nothing."

"You said something about a card."

"Yes, sir; it was sent in to me tonight while I was with my sick friend—man wanted to see him on business and insisted upon coming in, and it was all I could do to put him off."

"Brood too much," the Judge repeated, after a brief interval of silence. "The mind mildews under any one thing that lies upon it long. A continuous joy might be as poisonous as a grief." He leaned forward with his head in his hands, and talked in a smothered voice.

"The sun is coming up," said Bodney. "Don't you think you'd better lie down?"

"You go to bed. Don't mind me."

"Believe I will. I am worn out, and I don't see how you can stand it as well as you do."

"In worry there is a certain sort of strength. Go to bed."

Bodney got up and went to the door, but turned and looked at the old man, bowed over with his fingers pressed to his eyes. The coming of the sun had driven the game further off into the night, and now the wretch's heart smote him hard. He could lift that gray head; into those dull eyes he could throw the light of astonishment, but they would shoot anger at him and drive him out of the house. If he could only win enough to replace the money taken from the safe, to give himself the standing of true repentance, he would confess his crime. Win enough! He could not conceive of getting it in any other way; all idea of business had been driven from his mind. He had no mind, no reason; what had been his mind was now a disease on fire, half in smoke and half in flame, but he felt that if he could get even, the fire would go out and the smoke clear away. The old fellow who turned moralist could have told him that he had for more than half a lifetime struggled to get even, that the poker fool is never even but twice, once before he plays and once after he is dead. And the scholar who had forgotten his grammar in the constant strain of the present tense would have assured him that the hope to get even was a trap set by the devil to catch the imaginative mind.

The Judge groaned, and Bodney took a step toward him, with his hands stretched forth as if he would grasp him and shake him into a consciousness of the truth, but the old man looked up and the young man faltered. "I thought you were going to bed, George."

"I am, sir."

"Then, why do you stand there looking at me?"

"I—I don't know," he stammered, in his embarrassment.

"Yes, you do know," said the Judge, giving him a straight and steady look. "You know that you are hanging about to plead the cause of your—your friend; but it is of no use. Friend! I would to God he had been my friend. Confess, now; isn't that the reason you are standing there?"

"You read my mind, Judge," said the wretch.

"Do I? Then read mine and go to bed."

As Bodney turned toward the door, he met William coming in. The old fellow carried his coat thrown across one arm and was trying to button his shirt collar. It was his custom to begin dressing at his bedside, grabbing up the first garment within reach, and to complete his work in the office, the basement, or even the back yard. "Hold on a minute," he said to Bodney. "Button this infernal collar for me." Bodney halted to obey. "Can't you take hold of it? Is it as slick as all that? Do you think I wear an eel around my neck? Confound it, don't choke the life out of me. Get away. I can do it better myself. Didn't I tell you to quit? Are you a bull-dog, that you have to hang on that way?"

Bodney trod heavily to his room. The old fellow threw his coat on the table and began to walk about, tugging at his collar.

"Do you think you can button it here better than in your own room?" the Judge asked, straightening up and looking at him. "Has this office been set aside as a sort of dressing parade ground for you?"

William was muttering and fuming. "I was Judge Lynch out West, once, and was about to set a horse-thief free, but just then I incidentally heard that he had sold collars and I ordered him hanged. Did you speak to me, John?"

"I asked you a question."

"I knew a Universalist preacher that changed his religion on account of a collar—swore that its inventor must necessarily go to the flames. What was the question you asked me, John?"

"One that would have no more effect on you than a drop of water on the back of a mole."

William buttoned his collar, tied his cravat, took a seat opposite his brother and looked hard at him. "John, I see that your temper hasn't improved. And you have got up early to turn it loose on me. Now, what have I done? Hah, what have I done?"

"I have never heard of your doing anything, William."

"That's intended as an insult. Oh, I understand you. You never heard of my doing anything. You haven't? You never heard of my electing two governors out West. You bat your eyes at the fact that I sent a man to the United States Senate. Why, at one time I owned the whole state of Montana, and a man who had never done anything couldn't —couldn't make that sort of showing."

"What did you do with the state?"

"What did I do with it? A nice question to ask a man. What did Adam do with the Garden of Eden?"

"You were not driven out of Montana, were you?"

"Driven out? Who said I was driven out?"

"But Adam was driven out of the garden."

"Oh, yes, of course. I merely spoke of the

Garden of Eden for the reason that Adam's claim on it was only sentimental, if I may call it such. I mean that I owned the good opinion of every man in the state. I could have had anything within the gift of the commonwealth."

"Then, why didn't you go to the Senate, or elect yourself governor? Why were you so thoughtless a prodigal of your influence?"

"That's a nice question to ask a man. Why didn't you buy an acre in this town that would have made you worth millions? Why didn't I go to the Senate? I had something else on my mind. Every man is not ambitious to hold office. There's something higher than politics. I was educated for a different sphere of action. I was, as you know, educated for a preacher, but my faith slipped from under me. But it is of no use to talk to you."

"Not much, William, I admit."

"But can't you tell me why this peculiar change has come over you? It worries me, and you know why."

The Judge made a gesture. "Don't—it's not that. My mind is perfectly sound."

"Then, what's the trouble?"

"I can't tell you."

"Am I ever to know?"

"I hope not."

"I don't see why you should give me the keen edge of your temper and not tell me the cause that led you to whet it against me."

"I have not whetted it against you—it has been whetted on my heart. Go away, William, and leave me to myself."

"I would if you were yourself, but you are not. There is something the matter with you."

"I grant that."

"And in it there is cause for alarm, both for you and for myself."

"Now, please don't allude to that again. My mind is perfectly sound, I tell you."

"And so one dear to us often declared."

The Judge got up. "I shall have to command you to leave this room."

"Then, of course, I'll go. Here comes your wife. Rachel, there is something radically wrong with John, and I advise you to send for the best physician in this town."

CHAPTER IX.

HEARD A GONG IN THE ALLEY.

More than once during the night had Mrs. Elbridge looked in upon her husband, to urge upon him the necessity for rest. But he had told her that he had on hand the most important case that ever came to him, declared that the life of a man depended upon his meditation; a new point in law was involved, and it would be a crime to sleep until his work was done. The governor of the state had submitted the question to him. And thus had she been put off, having no cause to doubt him; but now she caught William's alarm. "My dear," said the Judge, when she approached him, "it seems that both you and my brother are struggling hard to misunderstand me. You know that I have never deceived you—you know that I would tell you if there were anything wrong. It is true that the death of my brother Henry has shocked me greatly—"

"But why don't you tell William? He ought to know. And it is our duty to tell him."

The old man, looking toward the door, held up his hand. "No, he must not be told—nor must anyone else. I have an object."

"But, my dear, I don't see—"

"I know you don't. And I cannot tell you—I can—can merely hint. It is a question of life insurance, and the company must not hear of his death till certain points are settled. William, as you know, while one of the best men in the world, has a slippery tongue. And, besides, he is in no condition now to hear bad news. It is a secret, but he is having trouble with his heart—under treatment. Let us wait till he is stronger."

"But, dear, is that a cause why you should frown so at Howard, and treat him with such contempt?"

He walked away from her, but she followed him and put her hand on his arm. They halted near the safe and stood in silence, he looking at the iron chest, she looking at him. The sound of a peddler's gong came from the alley, and he sprang back from the safe and dropped heavily down upon a chair. Florence was heard talking to someone, and Mrs. Elbridge called her, and at this the old man brightened. Florence was his recourse, his safeguard, and when she came in he greeted her with something of his former heartiness.

"Florence, they are worried about me. Tell them that they have no cause."

The young woman's face was bright with a smile, but it was a light without warmth, a kindly light intended to deceive, not the Judge, but his wife. Mrs. Elbridge looked at her husband and was astonished at the change in him. She could not understand it, but she was not halting to investigate causes. "You are our physician, Florence," she said. "But you must bring your patient under better discipline. He didn't go to bed at all last night."

"Then I shall have to reprimand him. Sir, why do you disobey my orders?"

The old man's attempt at a smile was but a poor pretense, but it deceived the eye of affection. "Because, Doctor, I had a most important case on hand; but it is about worked out now, and I will in the future have more regard for your instructions."

They talked pleasantly for a time, and then Mrs. Elbridge went out, leaving the Judge and Florence in the office; but no sooner was the wife gone than the husband began to droop; and the light of the forced smile faded from the countenance of the young woman. She looked at the Judge and her face was stern. "We are hypocrites for her," she said, nodding toward the door through which Mrs. Elbridge had just passed.

"Yes, to protect the tenderest nature I have ever known. She could not stand such a trouble. It would kill her."

"She would not believe your story."

"Yes, she would. Unlike you, she could not be infatuated with the blindness of her own faith. She loves her son, but she knows me—loves me. She could not doubt my eyes. What," he said, getting up with energy and standing in front of Florence, "you are not debating with yourself whether or not to tell her, are you? Can you, for one moment, forget your oath—an oath as solemn and as binding as any oath ever taken? You, surely, are not forgetting it."

"No, but I ought to. My heart cries for permission to tell Howard. His distress reproaches me."

"But your oath."

"Oh, I shall not forget it, sir," she said, almost savagely. "But, it was not generous of you—not generous."

"What wasn't?"

"Swearing me to secrecy. You took advantage of what you conceive to be my honor, my strength of character; and you would have me break his heart by refusing to marry him. You have a far-reaching cruelty."

"Florence—my daughter, you must not say that. You know why I would keep you from marrying him. Have I been a judge all these years, to find that I am now incapable of pronouncing against my own affections and my own flesh and blood? I am broader than that."

"You mean that you are narrower than that. It is noble to shield those whom we love."

"No, it is selfish. You are a woman, and therefore cannot see justice as a man sees it."

"My eyes may not be clear enough to see justice, but they have never beheld a vision to—"

"Don't, Florence—now, please don't. You know how I held him in my heart; you know that no vision could have driven him out. But it is useless to argue. I have knowledge and you have faith. Knowledge is brightest when the eye is opened wide; faith is strongest when the eye is closed."

And thus she replied: "Ignorant faith may save a soul; knowledge alone might damn it."

"Very good and very orthodox, my child; a saying, though, may be orthodox, and yet but graze the outer edge of truth."

"But if there be so little truth in things orthodox, why should there be such obligation in an oath?"

"Ah, you still have that in your mind. Look at me. I hold you to that oath. Will you keep it?"

"Yes, but if I did not believe that within a short time something might occur to clear this mystery, I would break it in a minute."

"And let your soul be damned?"

"Now, *you* are orthodox. Yes, I would break it. But I will wait, in the belief that something must occur."

"There is no way too tortuous for a faith to travel," the old man murmured, but then he bethought himself that to encourage waiting was a furtherance of this humane plan of protection, and then he added: "Yes, wait; we never know, of course. Something might occur. But make me a promise, now in addition to your oath—that if, finally, when nothing does occur and you are resolved to break it, that you will first come to me."

"I will make that promise."

Agnes tripped in with a tune on her lips. The Judge wondered why George Bodney had not fallen in love with her. She was bright enough and pretty enough to ensnare the heart of any man. But Bodney was peculiar, and susceptibility to the blandishments of a bewildering eye was not one of his traits; his nature held itself in reserve for a debasing weakness. Agnes asked Florence why everyone seemed to drift unconsciously into that mouldy old office. Florence did not know, but the Judge said that it was attractive to women because it was their nature to find interest in the machinery of man's affairs. Business was the means with which man had established himself as woman's superior, and there was always a mystery in the appliances of his workshop.

"What nonsense, Mr. Judge," said Agnes. "It is because there is so much freedom in here. You can't soil anything in here—never can in a place where men stay." Howard passed the door, and the Judge's face darkened. Florence looked at him and her eyes were not soft.

"Now, what are you frowning at, Mr. Judge?" said Agnes. "Do you mean that I haven't told the truth?"

"You always tell the truth, Agnes."

"No, I don't. I told Mr. Bradley a fib—a small one, though; a little white mouse of a fib. But you have to tell fibs to a preacher."

"It is the way of life. Fibs to a preacher and lies to a judge," said the old man.

"Lies *for* a judge," Florence spoke up.

"What's the matter with everybody!" Agnes

cried, looking from one to another. "You people talk in riddles to me. I'm not used to it. And, Florence, you are getting to be so sober I don't know what to do with you. You and the Judge are just alike. What's the matter with everybody? Mr. Howard mumbles about the house and Mr. Bodney acts like a man with—with the jerks, whatever that is, for I don't know. There, I'm glad breakfast is ready. Come on, Mr. Judge."

CHAPTER X.

WILLIAM AGREED WITH THE JUDGE.

The Judge took his accustomed seat at the head of the breakfast table, Howard on his right and Bodney's vacant chair at his left; but there was no disposition on the part of the worry-haunted father to enter into conversation with the son. Howard was talkative; his mind might have been termed dyspeptic instead of digestive. The books, stories, sketches, scraps that he read, ill-stored, appeared as a patchwork in his talk. He spoke of a French author, and Florence saw the Judge wince. She was sitting beside Howard, and she pulled at his coat sleeve as a warning to drop the disagreeable name. He understood and changed the subject, but the fire had been kindled.

"It is no wonder that the French could not whip the Germans," said the Judge, not addressing himself to Howard, but to the table. "It was the literature of France that weakened her armies. Morality was destroyed, and without morality there can be no enduring courage."

"I think Victor Hugo is just lovely," said Agnes.

The Judge nodded assent. "A great genius— and, by the way, he said that there were but three men worthy to be estimated as memorable in all the history of this life—Moses, Shakespeare and Homer. He belonged to older and better France, at the dying end of her greatness. And you will observe that he did not include a Frenchman in his list."

"But I warrant you," said Howard, "that in his secret mind he put himself at the head of it."

The Judge looked at him. "Warrants issued by you, sir, are not always returnable accompanied by the facts."

"No, I wouldn't issue a warrant for the arrest of a fact. Truth ought to be at large."

Florence glanced at the Judge and saw him slowly close his eyes and slowly open them. "You think Hugo lovely," said the old man, speaking to Agnes. "But what do you think of Zola?"

"I don't know anything about him. But some of the girls said he was horrid," she answered.

"It is a good thing for you that you don't know anything about him, and it reflects credit upon the judgment of the girls who pronounced him horrid," said the Judge. "His influence upon his own country, and upon this country, too, has been most pernicious."

William was usually most prompt at meal time, but now he was for some unaccountable reason delayed; but he came in just as the Judge closed his remark concerning Zola, sat down and began to tuck a napkin under his chin. The Judge had more than once hinted his displeasure at this vulgarity, but his brother continued to practice it, not without heeding the hint, but with a defense of his custom. He had elected governors, and was not to be ruled into discomfort by a woman who had written a book on etiquette. He knew politeness as well as the next man or next woman, for that matter. Many a time had he seen Senator Bascomb, who owed his election to him, sit down to table in his shirt sleeves, with a napkin tucked into his bosom, and Washington City was compelled to acknowledge him a man of brains. The Judge stared at William, and was doubtless about to repeat his hint, when Florence said something to attract his eye, and shook her head at him.

"What have we under discussion this morning?" said William, squaring in readiness to defend himself, for he ever expected an attack.

"French literature," Howard answered.

"French fiddlesticks," William replied. "There is no French literature. They have slop that they call literature."

"I thank you, William," said the Judge, forgetting the napkin. This was received by the former owner of Montana as proof that the Judge's ill-nature had been cured; and, bowing, he pulled the napkin from about his jowl and spread it upon his knees. And then arose a spirited discussion between the political Warwick and Howard, the former snatching a cue from his brother, affirming that the influence of France had always been bad, the latter maintaining that France had civilized and cultivated the modern world. Florence pulled at Howard's coat sleeve; and the Judge, observing her, and irritated that she was moved to employ restraint, threw off all attempt at an exercise of his patience. "Let him proceed!" he roared, and everyone looked at him in surprise. "Let him proceed to the end of his disgraceful advocacy of corruption. But I will not stay to hear it." And, getting up, he bowed himself out.

"Howard," said Mrs. Elbridge, "you ought not to talk about things that irritate your father. He is not well."

"You are wrong, Howard, to oppose him," Florence spoke up.

"I suppose I am," the young man admitted, "but he has always taught me to form an opinion of my own and to hold it when once well formed, and until recently he seemed pleased at what he termed my individuality and independence. But now I can't do or say a thing to please him. I'm no child, and not a fool, I hope; then, why should I be treated as if I had no sense at all? What have I done that he should turn against me? He treats everyone else with consideration and respect. He even has toleration of Uncle William's dates," he added, mischievously thrusting at the old fellow for the recent stand he had taken, knowing that, with him, it was the policy of the moment rather than the conviction of the hour.

"What!" exclaimed William, with a bat of eye and a swell of jaw. "Turned loose on me, have you? Well, I want to tell you, sir, that I won't stand it. I am aware that my forbearance heretofore may have misled you with regard to the extent of my endurance, but I want to say that you have made a mistake. I am treated with consideration and respect everywhere except in this household, and I won't stand it, that's all."

"Thank you," Howard replied.

"Thank me! Thank me for what?"

"You said, 'that's all,' and I thank you for it."

Mrs. Elbridge interposed with a mild and smiling admonition. She shook her finger at Howard. "Let him go ahead, Rachel," the old fellow spoke up. "Let him go ahead as far as his strength will permit him. He's—he's set himself against us, and as he runs riot in the privilege of the spoiled heir, why, I guess we'll have to stand it—as long as we can. Of course, there'll come a time when all bodily and moral strength will fail us, but until then let him go ahead. Yes, has set himself against us."

"Us, did you say, Uncle Billy? You are evidently one of the us. Who's the other?" Howard asked, immensely tickled, for the warmth of the family joke was most genial to him.

"I don't want any of your Uncle Billying. I always know what to expect when you begin that."

"I began it the other night and ended by giving you a meerschaum pipe, didn't I?"

"Oh, meerschaum. Chalk—if there ever was a piece used by a tailor to mark out the angles of a raw-boned man—that pipe's chalk. You could no more color it than you could a door-knob."

"A friend of mine brought it from Germany, Uncle Billy."

"Did he? He brought it from a German beer

garden, where they peddle them in baskets and sell them by the paper bag full, like popcorn. I had my suspicions at the time."

"But you were willing to run the risk of acceptance because your pipe was so strong."

The old fellow put down his knife and fork and, straightening up, looked at Howard as if he would bore him through. "I deny your slander, sir."

"So do I," said Howard.

"You do what?"

"Deny the slander—unless there is slander in truth."

"Howard, you remind me of a cart-horse, treading on his trace chains. You remind me—I don't know what you remind me of."

"Of a cart-horse, you said."

Again Mrs. Elbridge admonished him not to irritate the old fellow, but did it so laughingly that he accepted it more as a spur than as a restraint; and Florence pulled at his sleeve, but more in connivance than in reproof. Agnes laughed outright. She declared that it was better than a circus. The old man turned his eyes upon her, giving her a long and steady gaze, and she whispered to Florence that even the pin-feathers of his dignity had begun to rise. "Better than a circus," he replied. "I don't see any similarity except that we have a clown." He winked at Mrs. Elbridge, as if he expected her to rejoice in what he believed to be a victory over the young man. Marriage may cripple a man's opportunities—in some respects it may restrict his range of vision, but it renders his near view much more nearly exact. Having never known the repressions of the married state—ignorant of the intellectual clearing-house of matrimony—William was blind to many things, and particularly to the fact that the mother hated him at that moment, though she smiled when he winked at her.

"Not much like modern circuses," Howard admitted. "They have a whole group of clowns, while we have but two, at most."

"Howard," said the old fellow, "do you mean to call me a clown?"

"Not a good one, Uncle William."

"Not a good one. Well, sir, I want to say that I'd make a deuced sight better one than you." When emphasis was put upon the word, it meant, with Uncle William, not the opprobrious, but the commendable. During his boyhood, to be a clown was to be greater than a judge, greater, if possible, than the driver of a stage-coach. In the old day, it was a compliment to tell a boy that he would make a good clown.

"I don't doubt you'd make a good clown, Uncle Billy. Aspiration is, within itself, a sort of fitness."

"What do you mean by that?"

"There is a certain genius in mere ambition," Howard went on. "If we yearn—and yearn, only, we come nearer to an achievement than those who don't yearn. Who knows that genius is not desire—just desire, and nothing more. I know a man over at St. Jo that can eat more cherries than any man in Michigan, not because he is larger than any of the rest, but because he has a broader appetite for cherries—more yearning."

William turned to Mrs. Elbridge. "Rachel, do you think he's lost what little sense he ever had."

"William," she said, "you must not talk to me that way. I won't put up with it, sir. I am sure he has as good sense as any—"

"Oh, if you are going to turn against me I guess I'd better go," he broke in, getting up. "I'll go to my brother. He at least can understand me."

The Judge was in the office. William entered, and, going up to the desk, began to rummage among some papers. "Trying to swim?" the Judge asked, looking up from a document spread out before him on the table.

"No, I'm looking for a cigar."

"I thought you were trying to swim."

William stepped back from the desk. "John, I didn't expect such treatment after our hearty agreement at the breakfast table. But it's what I get for taking sides. The neutral is the only man that gets through this life in good shape."

"And is that the reason, William, that you didn't preach—didn't want to take sides against the devil?"

"If I'm not wanted here, I can go to my own room."

"I wish you would. I am expecting an old client."

"Oh, I can go."

"Can you?"

"John, your irritability has irritated everybody on the place. You have poisoned our atmosphere. I will leave you."

"Thank you," said the Judge, examining the document before him. After a time, and still without looking up, he added: "Still here?"

"I have just come in, sir," said Howard. The Judge looked up.

"I thought it was William."

"He has just gone out. And I have come to beg

your pardon for what I said at breakfast. I didn't mean to worry you; I—"

"It is unnecessary to beg my pardon, sir."

"I hope not." He moved closer, with one hand resting upon the table. "Father, something is wrong, and—"

"Most decidedly."

"But won't you please tell me what it is? If the fault is in me and I can reach it I will pull it out. I could bear many crosses, but your ill-opinion is too heavy."

The old man looked up at him. "To your lack of virtue you have added silly reading."

"But I am playing in a farce worse than any I have ever read. Be frank with me. You have taught me frankness."

"And tried to teach you honesty."

"Yes, both by precept and example. But what is to come of it all when you treat me this way? Why don't you go to some springs?"

"Why don't you leave me to myself?"

"I am almost afraid. You rake up enmities against me when you are alone, it seems; and you pour them out upon me when we meet. Why is it?"

The Judge waved him off. "Go away," he said.

CHAPTER XI.

THE OLD OFFICE.

The office in La Salle Street was in an old-fashioned building, with heavily ornamented front. The room was large, high of ceiling, with a grate and a marble mantlepiece. It was on the first floor, after the short flight of iron steps leading from the pavement. Once it had been active with business, but now few clients found their way into its dingy precincts. Occasionally some old-timer would come in, but upon seeing Howard or Bodney, faces offensively young to him, would go out again, sighing over the degeneracy of the day. The young men had often advised a change of quarters, apartments in a steel building, but the Judge would not consent. The old room was sentiment's heritage. Many a famous man had trod the rough carpet on the floor; many a time had the dry eye of the tired lawyer watered at the wit of Emery Storrs; and Ingersoll, warm with fellowship and wine, walking up and down, had poured out the overflow of his magic brain. How intellectual were its surroundings then, and now how different! The great advocate was gone, and in his stead sat the real-estate lawyer, emotionless, keen-eyed, searching out the pedigree of a title to a few feet of soil—narrow, direct, dyspeptic, money-dwarfed.

After leaving home, Howard went straightway to the down-town office, and there, amid the dust raised by the negro who was sweeping, he found Goyle, waiting for Bodney. "I have taken possession," said Goyle.

"All right. And you are taking more dust than is good for you."

"I don't mind that. Where is Bodney?"

"He hadn't got up when I left home. He was up all night with a sick friend, I believe, and is not likely to be down before the afternoon."

Goyle looked at his watch. "I will come in again about three o'clock. How is business with you?" He did not get up.

"The business of waiting is good. It is about all a young lawyer need expect." Howard sat down, telling the negro to leave off sweeping; and Goyle, leaning back, put his feet upon the window ledge. He was never in haste to leave. It was one of his sayings that he was looking for a soft seat, and he appeared now to have found one. He gazed out into the rumbling thoroughfare, at men of all ages passing one another, pushing, jamming, limping, some on crutches, some tottering, some strong of limb, all with eager faces. "Rushing after the dollar," said Goyle.

"Or fleeing from necessity," replied Howard.

"Yes, and hard pressed by the enemy. But they have made their enemy powerful—have built up their necessities. Once a shadow lay upon the ground, a harmless thing; but they breathed hot breath upon it and it became a thing of life, jumped up and took after them. I hate the whole scheme." He waved his hand, and Howard sat looking at him—at the hair curling about his forehead, at his Greek nose; and he wondered why one so seemingly fitted for the chase should express such contempt for it. He spoke of it, and Goyle turned toward him with a cold smile. "You have heard," said he, "of the fellow who would rather be a cat in hell without claws. Well, that's what I am, and where I am when thrown out there." He nodded toward the street, and then lazily taking out a cigarette, lighted it.

"I don't believe that," said Howard. "I believe that you are well fitted, except, possibly, by disposition. You lack patience."

"Patience! It doesn't admit of patience. Do those fellows out there look patient?"

"A man may run and be patient."

"And he may also run and be a fool."

"Or be a bigger fool and not run. I am a believer in the world—in man."

"I'm not," said Goyle. "I know that the world is a trap and that man is caught. Puppies play, but the old dog lies down. He knows that life is a farce."

"The old dog lies down, it is true," Howard replied, "but he dreams of his youth and barks in his dream."

"And calls himself a fool when he awakes. It is the same with the old man. There comes a time when he loses confidence even in those who are nearest him." Out of the sharp corner of his eye he shot a glance at Howard and saw his countenance change. An old man, shriveled and wretched, with feather dusters for sale, came shambling into the room. Goyle glanced at him, and when he was gone, turned to Howard and said: "Ask his opinion of the world. He is your old dog who dreamed and barked in his dream."

"Goyle, I don't like the position you take. My experience and my reading teach me better."

Goyle glanced at him again. "Your reading, because what you read was written to flatter hope—to sell. Your experience is not ripe. It is not even green fruit. It is a bud. Oh, of course there are some old men, your father, for instance, who—"

"Well, what about him?"

"Nothing, only he is by nature fitted to smile at everything."

Howard got up, went over to a bookcase, took down a book, put it back, went to the open door, and stood there looking at a doctor's sign, just across the hall. Goyle got up with a yawn, came walking slowly toward the door, and Howard, hearing him, but without looking round, stepped aside to let him pass out. In the hall he halted to repeat that he would return during the afternoon.

"You have the privilege to come and go as often as you like, being George's friend," said Howard, "but, so far as you and I are concerned, I don't think we are suited to each other."

Goyle laughed and stepped back a pace or two. "Why, on account of my nonsense just now? That was all guff; I didn't mean it. It is the easiest thing in the world for a man to condemn the whole of creation, and I talk that way when my mind is too dull to act. Why, I am going out now to knock an eye tooth out of the wolf."

"And you didn't mean what you said about old men?"

"Not a word of it."

"Why did you happen to speak of my father?"

"Merely to refute what I had said about old men in general. Well, so long."

Howard went into the doctor's office, as musty a den as ever a fox inhabited. The physician was an old man, who had no future and who prescribed in the past. During the best years of his life he had dozed or talked under the influence of opium, so given to harmless fabrication when awake that it followed him into his slumber, snoring a lie; now cured of the habit but not of the evil it had wrought. When Howard entered the old man was reading a medical journal of 1849, and he glanced up disappointed to see the visitor looking so well. He had met Howard many a time, but his memory was short.

"Ah, come in, sir. Have a seat. You are—let me see.

"My office is just across the hall."

"Yes, yes, I remember. You are in the—the brokerage business. And your name is—"

"I am trying to be a lawyer. Elbridge is my name."

"Of course it is. I used to know your father—was called in consultation just before he died."

"Then it must have been since I left the house this morning."

"Ah, let me see. Elbridge—the Judge. I'm wrong, of course. It was Elsworth. How is your father?"

"That's what I wanted to talk about, and I am sorry that you do not recall him more vividly. I wanted to ask your opinion."

"Why, now I know him as well as I know myself. What is it you wish to consult me about? His health?"

"Well, I hardly know how to get at it. You know he has been a very busy man—working day and night for years; and I wanted to ask if a sudden breaking off isn't dangerous—that is, not exactly dangerous, but likely to induce a change in disposition?"

The doctor looked wise, with his hand flat upon the medical journal, and as it had been printed in the drowsy afternoon of a slow day, seemed to inspire caution against a quick opinion.

"I hold, and have held for years," said he, "that a

complete revolution in a man's affairs, sudden riches or sudden poverty—the er—the withdrawing of vital forces necessary to a continuous strain, is a shock to the system, and therefore deleterious. It is unquestionably a fact, not only known to the medical fraternity, but to ordinary observation, that incentive in the aged is a sort of continuance of youth, in other words, to make myself perfectly clear, the impetus of youth when unchecked, goes far into old age—when the pursuit has not been changed; and therefore a sudden halting is bad for the system. Is your father's health impaired?"

"I can't say that it is. He appears to be strong, but his temper is not of the best—toward me. Toward the others he is just the same."

"Ah, not unusual in such cases. It so happened that a sudden change must have taken place in him, and as you were doubtless the first one to come in contact with him after the change, his—his displeasure, if I may be permitted the term, fell upon you."

"But I was not the first one."

"Um, a complication. I shall have to study that up a little. Perhaps I'd better see him."

"Oh, no, don't do that. It really amounts to nothing. I consulted you because you were well acquainted with him. And I am now inclined to think that I have made more of it than it really is. How are you getting along?" Howard asked, to change the subject.

"Never better, sir, I am pleased to say. Of course medicine has degenerated, splitting up into all sorts of specialties, but there are a few people who don't want to be humbugged. Well, I am glad you called," he added as Howard turned to go. "Give my regards to your father."

Howard returned to the office, took up a book which held in closer affinity the laws of verse than the laws of the land, and lying down upon a leather lounge, was borne away by the gentle tide of a rhythmic sea.

CHAPTER XII.

WALKED AND REPENTED.

A man can be more repentant when he walks than when he rides. The world's most meditative highway is that road which we are told is paved with good intentions; and strolling along it, our determination to reform becomes stronger at each step until—until something occurs to change it all. Bodney walked down town. And for the first time in his life he fancied that he found the very bottom of his mind, and thereon lay a resolution, an oath self-made, self-sworn to tell Howard the truth and to take the consequences no matter what they might be. He had intended, upon getting out of bed to make his confession to the old gentleman, and he would have done so, he fully believed, had not the Judge been engaged with a client. But perhaps after all it would better serve the purposes of justice to confess to Howard. He was the one most deeply injured. Yes, he would go at once to Howard and tell him the truth. It would of course involve

Goyle, but he ought to be involved; he was a scoundrel. Perhaps they might both be sent to the penitentiary. No matter, the confession must be made. He passed the building wherein the night before he had agonized under the frown of hard luck; he halted and looked into the entry-way, at the stairs worn and splintered by the heavy feet of the unfortunate. Some strange influence had fallen upon him, some strength not gathered by his own vital forces had come to him, and now he knew that no longer could he be a slave held by chains forged in that house of bondage. As he turned away he met a man who had been in the game the night before. His face was bright and he did not look like a slave.

"How did you come out?" Bodney asked.

"I was ninety in when you left, and I pull out sixty winner."

"You did? You were losing when I left."

"Yes, but they can't beat a man all the time. I tell you it would put me in the hole if I didn't win. I owe at three or four places, and I go around today and pay up."

Then, with a feeling like a sudden sickness at the stomach, came the recollection of the druggist and the preacher, obligations not to be discharged that day. Long after the moral nature has been weakened, the poker player may continue to respect his own word, or rather he may not respect it himself but may desire others to do so. Unless his income is large he must operate mainly upon borrowed capital, and breaking his word cripples his resources. And then, after having lost, there is a self-shame in having borrowed, a confession of weakness. He condemns himself for not having had strength enough to quit when he found that there was no chance to get even. "There never is a chance to get even," Bodney mused as he walked on toward the office. "The old fellow who has worn himself out at the cursed game says so and I believe it." I will tell Howard—nothing shall shake my resolution. I will simply cut my throat before I'll sink myself further in this iniquity. By nature I am not dishonest. If I hadn't met that fellow Goyle I might—but I'll not think of him. Now that fellow didn't play any better cards than I did, was nearly a hundred in and pulled out sixty ahead. And he has paid his debts while I must dodge. I wonder how much I have lost within the past two months. On an average of fifty dollars a sitting. That won't do. I had money enough to—but I won't think about it—won't do any good, and besides it is over with now."

He found Howard in the office writing. "A brief?" said Bodney, sitting down.

"In one sense—short meter," Howard replied.

"What, poetry?"

"Rhyme. I come by it naturally, you know. Have you heard from your friend today, the one you sat up with?"

"Yes, he's better."

"Goyle was here—said he'd be back this afternoon."

"Didn't leave any money—didn't say what he wanted, did he?"

"No. I think he wants to talk more than anything else. He is a smart fellow, George, but I am beginning to find fault with him. I don't like his principles."

"Perhaps he has none," Bodney replied.

"What, have you begun to—"

"Oh, no, I merely said that."

"That's the way he talks—makes a statement and then declares he didn't mean it. By the way, I'm going to get out of this office. There's no use staying here. If father wants to keep it, let him; but you and I ought to be in a more modern building. We have played at the law long enough. What do you say?"

"I don't know but you are right. I would like to do something. Has anyone else called?"

"Yes, Bradley was here."

"Bradley! What did he want?"

"He didn't say what he wanted."

"What did he say?"

"He inquired about your friend—the divinity student."

Bodney was silent, and to him it seemed that he was groping about in his own mind, searching for his resolution, but he could not find it. The preacher might have asked about the divinity student, the wretch mused, but of course he wanted ten dollars; and what if it should be known at the house that he had borrowed the money?

"Howard, can you let me have twenty-five dollars?"

"What, haven't you—you any money?"

"None that I can get hold of. I haven't said anything about it, but the fact is, I have invested in suburban lots, and can make a good profit any time I care to sell out, but I don't want to sell just now."

"Ah, business man, eh?" said Howard, crumpling the paper which he had covered with rhymes and throwing it into the waste basket. "Well, I am

Bodney took the money.

going to do something of that sort myself. I am glad you told me. Yes, I'll let you have twenty-five. I have just about that amount with me."

Bodney took the money and seized his hat. "If Goyle comes in, tell him I don't know when I'll be back. By the way, do you suppose Bradley went home?"

"Yes, I think so—in fact, he remarked that he was going home to do some work. Why?"

"Nothing, only he seemed interested in the young fellow I sat up with—wanted to go with me to see him, in fact."

With a determination to pay the druggist and to go at once to Bradley's house, Bodney left the office, still wondering, though, what had become of his resolve to make a confession to Howard. But he would fortify himself against trivial annoyances and then, morally stronger, he could confess. As he was crossing the street he thought of the fellow who had won sixty dollars. "No better player than I am," he mused. "He hung on, that's all. Now, when I pay the preacher and the druggist I'll have five dollars left. And with that five dollars I might win out. If I had held to my resolution not to stay in on so many four flushes I might have won out anyway. But the other fellows filled flushes and straights against me. Why couldn't I against them? Simply because it wasn't my day. But this may be my day. My day must come some time. As that fellow said, 'they can't beat a man all the time.' Why not go to the club first? Then, if I win, I can easily meet my obligations."

He went to the club. The game was full, but a "house" player got up and gave him a seat. He bought ten dollars' worth of chips, and the first hand he picked up was three queens. The pot was opened ahead of him and another man came in. Bodney raised; they stood it, and drew one card each. To disguise his hand, Bodney drew one, holding up a six. He caught a six. The opener bet a white chip. The next man raised him three dollars. Bodney raised all he had. The opener laid down; the other man studied. "Is it that bad?" he asked, peeping at the tips of his cards. Bodney said nothing; his blood was tingling, but in his eyes there was a far-away look.

"It's up to you, Griff," said an impatient fellow.

"Yes, so I see; but I'm playing this hand. Raised it and drew one card, then raised a one-card draw. Well, I've got to call you."

"Queen full."

"Beats a flush. Take the hay."

And now Bodney's troubles all were luminous. The wine of the game flowed through his veins and made his heart drunk with delight. He held a pat flush, won a big pot and felt a delicious coolness in his mind, the chamber wherein he had groped through darkness, searching for the lost resolution. But now it was light, and was crowded with charming fancies. He bubbled wit and simmered humor, and the look-out man said, "you bet, he's a good one." His stack was building so high that he could hardly keep from knocking it over—did overturn it with a crash, and a loud voice called to the porter: "Chip on the floor." The man attendant upon the desk came over, put his hand on Bodney's shoulder and said: "Give it to 'em; eat 'em up."

In the game there was a mind-reader, and they called him Professor. In his "studio" he told marvelous things, brought up the past and read the future. Hundreds of persons consulted him, race-track men looking for tips, board of trade men wanting to know the coming trend of the market; and in the twilight came the blushing maiden to ask if her lover were true. In deepest secret you might write a dozen questions, put them in your pocket and button your coat, but the Professor could read them. He was unquestionably a mind-reader—till he sat down to play poker—and then his marvelous powers failed him. The most unintuitive man at the table could beat him. Bodney slaughtered him. "Can you make those things every time?" said the Professor, calling a three-dollar bet.

"Not every time," Bodney replied, spreading a straight, "but I made it this time."

"You can make them every time against me. You are the luckiest man I ever saw. Do you always win?"

"I have lost more within the last two months than any man that comes up the stairs."

"That's right," said the look-out.

One wretched fellow, who had been struggling hard, got up broke. He strove to appear unconcerned, but despair was written on his face. As he walked across the room toward the door the man at the desk called to him. He turned with the light of a vague hope in his eye. In consideration of his hard luck was the house about to stake him? "Have a cigar before you go," said the man at the desk. The light went out of the wretch's eye. He took the cigar and drooped away, to beg for an extension from his landlord, to plead with the grocer, to lie to his wife.

WALKED AND REPENTED.

At six o'clock Bodney cashed in one hundred and four dollars. He would eat dinner with them, but he would not play afterward. He had tried that before. His eye-tooth had not only been cut; it had been sharpened to the point of keenest wisdom. While he was at the dinner table Goyle came in and took a seat behind him.

"Understand you sewed up the game," said the master.

"I've got just about enough to pay up what I owe," replied the slave.

"Come off. Let me have twenty."

"I can't do it—swear I can't. I owe all round town. I let you have ten yesterday, you know."

"That's all right. You'll get it again—you know that. Let me have twenty."

"I can't possibly do it."

But he did. Goyle got up and walked out into the hall with him, put his hand on his arm and stood a long time, talking, gazing into his eyes. So Bodney gave him the money and hastened away, his spirits somewhat dampened. But his heart was still light enough to keep him pleased with himself. Luck had surely turned. He would win enough to replace the money taken from the safe, and then he would make a confession. But, that fellow Goyle! What was the secret of his infatuating influence? How did he inspire common words with such power, invest mere slang with such command? But his influence could not last; indeed, it was weakening. And when thus he mused his heart grew lighter. "He couldn't make me aid and abet a robbery now," he said. "I would turn on him and rend him. Let him take the money. The debt is now large enough to make him shun me." With a smile and a merry salutation he stepped into the drug store, and handed the druggist ten dollars, apologizing for not having called during the day, but he had been busy and did not suppose that it would make any particular difference. The druggist assured him that it did not. Good fortune in its many phases may be taken as a matter of course, but the return of borrowed money is nearly always a surprise. The druggist gave him a cigar.

"Thank you," said Bodney. "By the way, have you an envelope and stamp?"

He found an envelope, but no stamp. A young woman who had held his telephone for ten minutes had bought the last one. It was of no consequence; Bodney could get one at the next corner. Tearing a scrap of paper out of his notebook and putting it upon a show case, he scribbled a few lines upon it, folded a ten dollar note in the paper, enclosed it in the envelope and directed it to Bradley.

"I guess that ought to be safe enough," he said.

"I don't know," replied the druggist.

"Well, I'll risk it. Again let me thank you for your kindness. It isn't often that I am forced to borrow, and wouldn't have done so last night but for—"

"Oh, that's all right. Come in again," he added, as Bodney stepped out. At the next corner he stamped his letter and went out to drop it into a box, but before reaching it was accosted by someone, the Professor whom he had slaughtered in the game.

"How did you come out?" Bodney asked.

"You broke me."

"Didn't you sit in after dinner?"

"For about three minutes—first hand finished me. I see you have a letter there with ten dollars in it."

"What! How do you know?"

"And a note written with a pencil."

"Why, that's marvelous. How do you do it?"

The Professor smiled. "It is the line of my business. Why don't you come up to my place some time? I can tell you many things."

It flashed through Bodney's mind that he might tell him many things, and he shrank back from him. "I will, one of these days," he said, and strode off without dropping his letter into the box. He put it into his pocket, intending to stop at the next corner, but forgot it. "Now, what?" he mused. "Believe I'll go home." He got on a car, but stepped off before it started. He went to a hotel, into the reading room, and took up a newspaper, but found nothing interesting in it. His thoughts were upon the game. In his mind was the red glare of a pat diamond flush. He could see it as vividly as if it had been held before his eye. Was it prophetic? He strolled out, not in the direction of the Wexton Club; but he changed his course, and was soon mounting the stairs. There was no seat, but the man at the desk said that there were enough players to start another game. The game was organized with four regulars, Bodney and another fool. The regulars took twenty dollars' worth of chips apiece; the two fools took ten, and within ten minutes Bodney was buying more. A man got up from the other table, and Bodney returned to his old seat, where he knew that luck waited for him. The desk man came over to him. "That other gentleman is number one," said he. Just then a new arrival took the seat which Bodney had vacated and number one called out: "Let him go ahead. I'll stay here." And there, sure enough, was the pat diamond flush. Wasn't it singular that he should have seen it glowing upon the surface of his mind? And wasn't it fortunate that the pot was opened ahead of him? He raised and the opener stayed and drew one card. He bet a white chip and Bodney raised. The opener gave him what was termed the "back wash," re-raised. Then the beauty of the flush began to fade. Could it be that the fellow—the very same offensive fellow, who had beaten him before—could have filled his hand? Or, had he drawn to threes and "sized" Bodney for a revengeful "bluff?"

"Well, I'll have to call you," said Bodney. He put in his money and the offensive fellow showed him a ten full.

"You always beat me."

"I do whenever I can."

"But you make it a point to beat me."

"Make it a point to beat anybody."

"Well, I don't want any abuse and I won't have it."

"Play cards, boys," said the look-out.

"What's the matter with you, worms?" said the offensive fellow, looking at Bodney.

"Play like brothers," spoke up the look-out.

At a little after eleven o'clock Bodney came down as heavy as a drowned man. His heart was full of bitterness. He cursed the world and all that was in it. He called on God to strike him dead. Then he swore that there could be no God; there was nothing but evil and he was the embodiment of it. But if he had only ten dollars he could win out. He had won, and it was but reason to suppose that he could win again. Any old player, imbued with the superstitions of the game, would have told him that to go back was to lose. "I'll go over and see that druggist again," he mused. "Strange that I have lived in this town all my life and don't know where to get money after eleven o'clock at night. I ought to have set my stakes better than that. And now, what excuse can I give for coming back to borrow again so soon? Perhaps he isn't there." Nor was he there. Bodney looked in with anxiety toward the show case behind which he expected to see his friend, and with contempt at the soda-water man. He thought of the envelope. He pictured himself standing there, smiling, a few hours before—and like an arrow came the recollection of the note directed to the preacher. He wheeled about, rushed across the street, jostling through the crowd which was still thick upon the sidewalk, raced around the corner, swam through another crowd, bounded across another street just in front of a cable train, and, breathless, panted up the stairway leading to the Wexton. Before touching the electric button he tore open the envelope, took out the money, destroyed the note; he touched the button and wondered if the black porter would ever come. Undoubtedly the game must have broken up. No, there was the black face, grim in the vitreous light. And there was a vacant seat, his old, lucky seat.

"Bring me ten," he called, as he sat down. And addressing the look-out, he asked if Goyle had been there. He had played a few pots after dinner, but had quit early.

"Did he win?"

"I think he win a few dollars. Said he had an engagement on the West Side."

"Leave me out," said a man, counting his imposing stack of chips. "Never mind, I'll play this one." A hand had been dealt him. "But I've got to go after this hand; oughtn't to stay as long as I do. Got to catch a train. Who opened it?"

"I did," replied a regular.

"Raise you."

"So soon? Well, I'll have to trot you. Tear me one off the roof."

"I'll play these," said the man who had to catch a train.

"You'd better take some. He won't come round again. Well, I'll chip it up to you."

"Raise you three."

The regular raised him back. The man who had to go raised, and the regular fired back at him, nor did the contest end here, but when it did end the regular spread an ace full to overcast with the shade of defeat three queens and a pair. And the man who had been in a hurry continued to sit there. At short intervals, during half an hour or more, he had snapped his watch, but he did not snap it now. Trains might come and trains might go, but he was not compelled to catch them; he lost his last chip, bought more, lost, and, finally, accepted carfare from the man at the desk. Bodney won, and the world threw off its sables and put on bright attire, and at two o'clock he thought of cashing in, though not quite even. He lacked just seventy-five cents— three red chips. He would play one more pot. He lost, and now he was two dollars behind, the pot having been opened for a dollar and twenty-five cents. Pretty soon he had a big hand beaten.

"I see my finish," he said.

"You can't win every pot," replied a railway engineer, who had failed to take out his train. "I have four pat hands beat and every set of threes I pick up. Serves me right. Pot somebody for a bottle of beer."

"You're on," replied the dealer, a comical-looking countryman, known as Cy. "Deal 'em lower, I can see every card," someone remarked; and just at that moment Cy turned over a deuce and replied: "Can't deal 'em much lower than that, can I?"

But who is this going down the stairs just as daylight is breaking? And why is he making such gestures? It is Bodney, and he is swearing that he will never play again.

CHAPTER XIII.

WANTED TO SEE HIS SON.

Howard had shared his father's sentiment with regard to the old office, for then the sky was clear, but now a cloud had come the atmosphere was changed. And on his way home to dinner, after a day spent without progress, he formed a resolve to tell the old gentleman that he needed a fresher and a brisker air than that blown about the ancient temple of lore. It ought not to hurt him now since he had begun to look upon his son with an eye so dark with censure. Even if his affection had been withdrawn his blood-interest must surely still remain, the young man mused; even though sentiment were dead, there must remain alive a desire to see him prosper, and to prosper in that old place was impossible. He believed that his father was losing his mind; years of dry opinion, of unyielding fact and the dead weight of precedent growing heavier, smothered his mental life.

The household, with the exception of the Judge,

was at dinner, and when Howard entered the dining room his mother arose hastily and came to meet him. "Your father wants to see you in the office," she said, and putting her hand on his arm, she added: "I don't know what he wants, but no matter what it is, please bear with him—don't say anything to annoy him."

"Has anything happened?" Howard asked.

"Something, but I don't know what. Someone called, I heard loud talking in the office, and after the caller had gone, your father came out and said that he wanted to see you as soon as you arrived. Be gentle with him, dear."

The old gentleman was sitting at his desk when Howard entered the office. He got up and for a time stood looking at the young man with no word of explanation. "Well, sir," he said, after a time, "what will you do next?"

"What have I done now?"

"No quibbling, sir. You know what you have done."

"I pledge you my honor I do not."

"Pledge me your what! Pledge me your old clothes, but not your honor."

"You wanted to see me, so mother says, and now I should like to know why."

"I suppose that you are so innocent that you can't even guess. Or is it that you are so forgetful of your deeds that you cannot remember? Why did you send that old fool out here?"

"Send an old fool out here! I didn't send anyone."

The old man took a step toward him with his finger uplifted. His eyes were full of anger and his finger shook, a willow in the wind. "How can you deny it? You sent old Dr. Risbin, the morphine eater, out here to see me."

"Oh, did he come out here? But I swear I did not send him. In fact, I told him not to come."

"Ah, and is that the reason he came—because you told him not to? He was never here before in his life, and why should he say that you sent him?"

"Because he is a poor old liar, I suppose. I admit that I saw him in his office and—"

"A gradual acknowledgment is better than no acknowledgment at all. Why did you see him in his office, or why did you speak of me?"

"Father, if you'll only be patient with me I will tell you. Your bearing toward me has been distressful. I was afraid that your mind—"

"Enough of that. My mind is sounder, sir, than

yours will ever be. But, suppose something were wrong. Is he the physician to consult? Why, his mind has been dead for years. Why did you consult him if it were not in contempt of me? I ask you why?"

"I was standing in the door of our office and happened to notice his sign just across the hall; and I thought that as he knew you well, I would speak to him. I soon saw that he didn't know what he was talking about, and when he suggested that he ought to see you, I told him no, and changed the subject. That's my offense, and I beg your pardon."

"I will try to believe you," said the Judge, sitting down. "Your office is down town. This one is mine."

"Yes, sir, and I will not intrude. I wouldn't have come in but you wanted—"

The Judge waved his hand. "Our business has been transacted."

"Yours has, but I have something to say. I don't want to occupy that musty old den any longer. It doesn't make any difference to me if there are a thousand javelins of wit sticking in the walls, or a thousand ghosts of oratory floating in the air, I can't make a living so long as I stay in it. I don't want to be of the past, but of the present. Your success was not a past but a present, and my present is as valuable to me as yours was to you."

"You are at liberty to get out of that office as soon as you like. But before you go, put up some sort of emblem expressive of your contempt of all its memories. Stuff out a suit of old clothes with straw, a scarecrow of the past, set it at the desk and call it—me."

"Please don't talk to me that way. I don't mean any disrespect—I want to establish myself on a modern footing. You know that Florence and I—"

"Don't speak of her."

"Why not? She is to be my wife."

"Not with my consent."

"Your consent is desirable, but not absolutely necessary. I don't mean this in impudence; I mean it merely to show my—our determination. I don't know why you should oppose our marriage, and I have no idea as to what extent you will oppose it, but I wish to say that no extreme will have any effect. You say that you are not ill; you swear that your mind is not affected, and yet you refuse to tell me the cause of your change toward me. I must have done something, either con-

The old man pointed toward the door, and Howard walked slowly out.

UNIV. OF
ALBERTA

sciously or unconsciously, and now again I beg of you to tell me what it is."

The old man leaned forward with his eyes bent upon the floor. "I have seen great actors, but this—go away, Howard. Leave me alone."

"Am I ever to know, sir?"

The old man pointed toward the door, and Howard walked slowly out. His mother stood in the hall. Her eyes were tearful, and taking his arm she held it as if she would say something, but liberated him, motioned him away, and went into the office. The Judge got up, forcing a change upon his countenance, smiled at her, took her hand and led her to a chair. "Now, don't be worried," said he. "I merely reprimanded Howard, as I had a right to do, for sending an old fool, who calls himself a doctor, out here to see me. That's all."

"But what did you mean by calling him an actor? What has he done that he should be acting now?"

"Nothing—nothing at all, I assure you."

"You said he was acting," she persisted.

"Perhaps I did, but I didn't mean it. Oh, yes, acting as if he didn't care for the memories of the old office."

"But, dear, something has come between you and Howard. What is it?"

"Between us, my dear? Surely not. We don't agree on all points; he has his opinions and I have mine; but there is no serious difference between us. Come, I will show you. He and I will eat dinner together."

He led her to the dining room, where Howard sat moodily looking at the table. He glanced up, and the Judge waved his hand with something of his old-time graciousness. "Any callers today, Howard?" he asked, sitting down.

"Goyle, whom I am beginning not to like, and Mr. Bradley."

"Whom you cannot help but like. A good man, conscientious and yet not creed-bound."

"He is building up a great church," said Mrs. Elbridge. "It is almost impossible to get a seat."

"Ah, I don't attend as regularly as I should," remarked the Judge, "but I am going to mend my ways. Howard, shall we go together soon?"

"I shall be delighted, sir."

"Then let us appoint an early day."

The father and the son laughed with each other, and to the mother it was as if new strings, to replace broken ones, had been put upon an old guitar, and she was happy merely to listen; but soon she was called away, attendant upon some

WANTED TO SEE HIS SON.

duty, and then a darkness fell upon the old man's countenance. "Enough of this," he said. And there was more than surprise in the look which Howard gave him—there was grief in it. "Then your good humor was assumed," he replied.

"We may assume good humor as we assume honesty—for policy," the Judge rejoined.

"I swear I don't understand you."

"Then don't strive to do so when your mother is present. At such times, take me as you find me."

"My pleasure just now was real. It is a grief to know that yours was not. I was in hopes that our difference, whatever it is, for I don't know, was at an end. You led me to believe so."

"Lay no store by what you suppose I lead you to believe. When our difference shall reach an end, if such a thing is possible, I will tell you."

"Then you acknowledge a difference."

"I have not denied it."

"And you will not tell what it is?"

"Now, you are mocking me. Ah, come in, my dear." Mrs. Elbridge had returned. "Yes, we will go to hear Bradley preach. And I warrant I can remember more of the sermon than you."

"Mr. Bradley is here now," said Mrs. Elbridge.

"Ah, is he? Did you tell him I would be in pretty soon?"

"He has come to see Agnes, I think. He asked for her."

"Ah, the sly dog. Well, he couldn't ask for a better girl. Are you going, Howard?"

"Yes, sir, to take a walk with Florence, if she cares to go."

The Judge frowned, but his wife did not notice it. Howard did, however, and was sorry that he spoke of his intention, but he had no opportunity to apologize, if indeed he felt an inclination to do so. It was a sorrow to feel that his father was set against him, but to know that he was trying to influence the girl was more than a sorrow—it was a grief hardened with anger. He found Florence and they went out together, walking southward.

"How soft the air is," she said.

"Nature is breathing low."

They walked on in silence beneath the cottonwoods and elms. Laughter, the buzz of talk and tunes softly hummed came from door-steps and porticos where families and visitors were gathered, to the disgust of Astors and flunkies from over the sea.

"Florence," said Howard, "before I came home this evening I was determined to move out of that old building down town, and to get an office in a modern building. But now I have decided upon something else."

"To remain there out of respect for your father and his memories?"

"No. To get away from this town—out West, to build a home for you. I hope you don't object."

"Object. I am pleased. I think it is the very wisest thing you could do. And as soon as you are ready for me, I will go."

He took her hand and held it till, passing under a lamp, near a group of persons on a flight of steps, he gently let it fall. "Yes, it is the wisest thing I can do. The law is altogether different from what it was when father was in his prime—the practice of it, I mean—and I don't believe I could ever build up here. Oh, I might. The fact is, I don't want to practice here. I am disheartened. The idea of a man, at his age, turning against—do you know what he holds against me, Florence?"

"Howard, you must not ask me."

"Must not ask you? Then you know."

"Please don't ask me."

They were in the light, amid laughter and the humming of tunes, and he waited till they reached a place where there was no one to hear, and then he said: "If you know and love me, it would be unnatural not to tell me."

"Howard, Peter may have denied his Lord, martyrs may have denied their religion, but you can't deny my love."

"No, I can't; but how can you keep from me a secret that concerns me so vitally? Do you suppose I could hold back anything from you?"

"Not if your mother were dead and you had taken an oath upon her memory?"

"Not if God were dead and I had sworn—"

"Howard, you must not talk that way."

He was holding her hand and he felt the ripples of her agitation. "I think I know your secret," he said. "You have cause to believe that his mind is giving way and you don't want to distress me by confessing it—have been sworn to silence, as if it could be kept hidden from me."

She admitted that she did not believe that his mind was sound, and he accepted it as the secret which she had at first held back, but her conscience arose against the deception of leaving him so completely in the dark. "Howard, you have often said in your joking way that I have the honor of a man."

"Yes, the honor of the Roman famed for honor. But honor can be cool, and I need something warmer, now—love. I am, as you know, deeply distressed at father's condition; it has changed nearly all my plans—every plan, in fact, except the one great plan—our plan. Mother begs me to be patient. But for what end, if there is to be no improvement in his treatment of me? I took a hint from Uncle William, not intended for me, that there has been insanity in the family. That's a comforting thought, now, isn't it? Why do you tremble so?"

"Because I believe that there is truth in Uncle William's hint."

"But it should not have any effect upon our plans —our marriage."

"I would marry you, Howard, if you were a maniac."

They were in the dark, and he put his arm about her. "Then, let the whole world go insane," he said.

The soft air murmured among the leaves of the cottonwood. A band of happy children danced about an organ grinder in the street. A fraudulent newsboy cried a murder in Indiana Avenue, and from afar came as if in echo, "All about the murder on Prairie Avenue."

"Howard, knowing me as you do, and supposing that I had not told all I know, and I were to ask you to wait, what would you say?"

"Not knowing you so well I would say, 'out with

it,' but knowing you, I would say, 'wait.' But what do you mean?"

"I mean to wait four weeks and no longer."

"Now you begin to mystify me. But we'll not think about it. I wonder what's the trouble with George. I never saw a fellow change so. I believe that fellow Goyle is having a bad influence on him. There is something uncanny about that chap. Did you ever notice his eyes? They have a sort of a draw, like a nerve. Have you noticed it?"

"I have noticed that I don't like him. He looks like a professional spiritualist."

"I guess he is in one sense—in slate writing—guess he has most everything put down on the slate."

"I don't know what you mean."

"Has everything charged that he can. He's a fraud, no doubt."

"Agnes says so."

"Oh, well, what Agnes says couldn't be taken as evidence. She sees a man and has a sort of flutter. If the flutter's pleasant the man's all right; if it isn't, he's all wrong."

"But there might be intuition in a flutter," she said.

"Yes, or prejudice. But George has always been

a good judge of men. He has excellent business sense—has invested in lots and can make a fair profit on them at any time he cares to sell. Shall we turn back here?"

Agnes and the preacher sat in the drawing room, she flouncing about on a sofa, and he dignified on a straight-back chair. It is rather remarkable that a preacher is more often attracted by a mischief-loving girl than by a sedate maiden; and this may account for the truth that ministers' sons are sometimes so full of that quality known, impiously, as the devil. In the early days of the English church, when the meek parson, not permitted to hope that he might one day chase a fox or drink deep with the bishop, and who was forced to retire to the servants' hall when the ale and the cheese cakes came on, had cause in secret to offer up thanks that not more than two of his sons were pirates on the high seas. And Bradley sat there watching a cotillion of mischief dancing in the eyes of the girl.

"You have never been connected with any church, have you?"

"Once," she replied, with a graceful flounce. "But I danced out."

"Danced out, did you say?"

"Yes. I got religion in the fall and lost it in the winter—by going to a ball and dancing."

"Why," said the preacher, slowly, patting his knee, "that did not cause you to lose it."

"Well, that's what they said, anyway. And I know I cried after I got home because my religion was gone."

"It is a crime to teach such rubbish."

"Then you don't think I lost it?"

"Surely not."

"Then I must have it yet," she cried, clapping her hands.

"Miss Agnes, your purity is of itself a religion."

"I don't know about that. I am wicked sometimes—I say hateful things."

"But there is no bitterness in your soul."

"I don't know, but I think there is, sometimes. I know once I wished that a woman was dead; but she was the meanest thing you ever saw. And she did die not long after that and I was scared nearly to death—and I prayed and sent flowers to the funeral. Wasn't that wicked?"

The preacher admitted that it was wayward, but he could not find it in his inflamed heart to call her wicked. She was too engaging, too handsome to be wicked. Nature could not so defame herself, he thought, though he knew that there was many a beautiful flower without perfume. But while settled love condemns, love springing into life forgives. "Wayward," said the preacher, "Perhaps thoughtless would be a better word."

"No, it wasn't thoughtless, because I was thinking hard all the time. Don't you get awfully tired studying up something to preach about?"

He smiled upon her. "All work in time becomes laborious, and that is why congregations desire young men—they want freshness. An old man may continue to be fresh, but his brain must be wonderful and his soul must be a garden of flowers. The wisdom of the old man often offends the young and tires the middle-aged; human nature demands entertainment, and the preacher who entertains while he instructs is the one who makes the most friends and the one who indeed does the most good. The unpoetic preacher is doomed; the gospel itself is a poem. The practical man may not read poetry, may not understand it; but he likes it in a sermon, for it breathes the gentleness and the purity of Christ. But poetry cannot be laborious, cannot be dry with studied wisdom, and therefore, when a preacher becomes a great scholar, he forgets his simple poetry and the people begin to forget him."

"My!" exclaimed the girl, "what a sermon you

have preached. And it's true, too, I think. I know we had an old man at our church—one of the best old men you ever saw—but they got tired of him. He—he couldn't hold anybody. Even the old men gaped and yawned. He was giving them dry creed. Well, a young man came along and preached for us. And it was like spring time coming in the winter. He made us laugh and cry. People like to cry—it makes them laugh so much better afterward. Well, the old man had to go."

"And after a time, the young man, grown old, will have to go. We must keep this life fresh; we must look for incentives to freshness. A preacher ought to be the most genial of men. And his wife ought to be genial; indeed, innocent mischief would not ill become her."

He looked at her, but she did not look at him. She was leaning back with her eyes half closed. "I hear Mr. Howard and Agnes coming," she said.

CHAPTER XIV.

A PROPOSITION TO MAKE.

Two weeks passed, and during the time Howard busied himself with the writing of letters to numerous real-estate men and postmasters in the West. Sometimes he would put down his pen to muse over what Florence had said, that she might tell him something after the lapse of four weeks, and more than once had he spoken to her with regard to what seemed to him as her vague information, but she had told him to wait. He knew her well enough not to persist. One of his earliest memories was a certain sort of stubbornness which formed a part of her character. She was gentle and lovable, but strong. He fancied that had she been reared in a different sphere of life she would have become a leader in the Salvation Army.

Bodney came to the office every day, but was so restless that he rarely remained long. Once he came to the door, saw the preacher within, and stole away without speaking. And one afternoon Howard heard him and Goyle tossing high words in the hall, but a few moments later they went out, arm in arm. One morning the Judge came in. "I didn't know but you had left this place," he said, standing near the door and looking about to search for the old memories, Howard mused.

"No, sir. The fact is I may not move to any other office in this town."

"In this town!" the old man repeated. "What other town is there?" To a Chicago man that ought to have established his complete soundness of mind. "I can give you credit for all sorts of—let me say, weakness—but I cannot see why you should be so foolish as to leave this city."

"You came at an early day," said Howard. "I might better my prospects by going to a town that is still in its early day."

"Um, and come back broke. You haven't stuffed that old suit of clothes yet."

"There's time enough for that, sir?"

"What! Then you really intend to do it?"

"Didn't you command me?"

"None of your banter." The Judge walked over to the old iron safe, with the names Elbridge & Bodney slowly rusting into the invisible past, put his hand upon it and stood there with his head bowed. From the street came the sharp clang of a fireman's gong, and the old man sprang back.

"There is a fire somewhere," said Howard.

"There is, sir; it is here," the Judge replied, putting his hand on his breast. Yes, it was now only too evident that his mind was diseased. The young man went to him, took his hand, looked into his eyes. "I beg of you to believe that my love for you is as strong as ever. I don't know how to humble myself, for you have taught me independence, but I would get down on my knees to you if—" The old man threw his hand from him and hastened from the room. In the hall he encountered the opium eating doctor. "Why, my dear Judge, I am surprised to see you out."

"And you will be still more surprised if you don't get out of my way."

"But won't you stop a while for old-time's sake?"

"I will do nothing, sir, but attend to my own affairs, and I request you to do the same."

"Of course, yes, of course. Well, drop in when you are passing."

The old doctor stepped up to the door of Howard's office. The young man stood confronting him. "I have thought over what you said the other day concerning your father, and have come to the conclusion that you are right," said the doctor. "There is something wrong with him."

"But I wish you wouldn't irritate him. And, by the way, why did you tell him that I told you to go out to the house?"

"Didn't you request me to go?"

"I certainly did not."

"Well, really, I misunderstood you. By the way, someone told me that you intended to give up this office. It is a better one than mine, having the advantage of a better view, and I don't know but I might take it."

"I am not going to give it up yet a while."

Bodney came into the hall and the old doctor shuffled into his own den. "I guess he wants to poison someone," said Bodney, nodding toward the doctor's office. "Anybody with you?" he asked.

"No," Howard answered, as they both stepped into the office. "Why?"

"Oh, I am getting so I don't want to see anybody. I feel as if I were a thousand years old," he added, dropping upon a chair.

"You don't look well, that's a fact. What seems to be the trouble?"

"I don't know. Liver, perhaps. Goyle been here today?"

A PROPOSITION TO MAKE. 173

"No, and I don't want him to come again. Now, look here, George, I believe that fellow has a bad influence on you. You are not the same man since you became so intimate with him. What's his business? What does he do?"

"I'd rather not talk about him, Howard."

"Then his influence must be bad. Turn him over to me the next—"

"No," Bodney quickly interposed. "Let everything go along as it is till the proper time and then—then I will attend to him. I am not in a position now to do anything, but one of these days I am going to tell you something that will open your eyes to the perfidy of man—man close to you. Don't say anything more now; I am crushed. I am—"

He leaned forward with his arms on a table and his head on his arms, his eyes hidden from the light. "Why, my dear boy," said Howard, going to him, touching him gently, "don't look at it that way. It is not so bad as that."

"It is worse," said Bodney, in a smothered voice. "It is worse than you can possibly picture it. And when I tell you, you will hate me as you never hated a human being on the earth. Don't ask me now, for I can't tell you. Just simply don't pay any attention to me. But I beg of you not to say a word at home. I have been led into hell, Howard, and there is no way out."

"Oh, yes, there is, my boy. There is the door through which you went in. Go out at it."

"I can't. You don't know."

"Are you in financial trouble? Has that fellow led you—"

"Worse than that, Howard. But I can't tell you now."

Once his long-delayed confession flowed to the very brim of utterance, but he forced it back and sat in silence. Howard went out and Bodney was thankful to be alone with his own misery; but he was not to be long alone—Goyle came in.

"Why, what's the matter, old chap? You seem to be in the dumps. Come, cheer up now. You've got no cause to be so blue? You don't see those fellows over yonder in the bank blue, do you? I guess not. And they are the biggest sort of robbers. I beat the horses today. And here's thirty of what I owe you. Oh, it's coming around all right. You can't keep a squirrel on the ground, you know."

"That's all right," replied Bodney, brightening as he took the bank notes. "Can't keep a squirrel

A PROPOSITION TO MAKE.

on the ground, but you can shoot him out of a tree."

"But we haven't been shot out of the tree yet. Things will begin to come our way now, you see if they don't. I've got a proposition to submit to you that will make us both rich—regular gold mine, with not a dull moment in it—life from beginning to end. I can't tell you now, but hold yourself in readiness for it. You can take that thirty and maybe win a hundred at the Wexton. In the meantime I'll be perfecting my plans. We shall need four or five agents, but I can get them all right, and if we don't live in clover a bumble bee never did. Now, don't you feel better? Look at me."

"Yes, I feel better."

"And don't you believe we'll pull out all right? Hah?" He put his hand on Bodney's shoulder and looked into his eyes.

"Yes, I do."

"Of course you do. We have been living in the night, but the sun is rising now. Let's go over to the Wexton and eat dinner."

"I ought to stay here till Howard comes back."

"Why, just to tell him you are going out? If you go out he'll know you are gone, won't he?"

"You go on and I will come pretty soon. I said

something to Howard just now that I want to correct."

"All right," said Goyle. "But come over as soon as you can."

When Howard returned he found Bodney idly drawing comic pictures on a sheet of paper. He looked at him in astonishment. "Why, what has happened?" Howard asked.

"My fit's passed, that's all. I must have talked like a wild man."

"I rather think you did. You alarmed me—said you were worse than ruined. What has occurred to change it all?"

Bodney laughed as he looked about, making ready to take his leave. He was beginning to be restless, for the fever was rising fast. He turned his eye inward to look for full hands and flushes.

"Nothing has occurred," said he. "The fit of melancholy has simply passed. That's all." He was moving toward the door.

"Don't be in a hurry," said Howard. "There is something I want to talk about."

"I haven't time now," Bodney replied. "I have thought of something that must be attended to at once."

"Just a moment, George. Hasn't Goyle been here?"

"Goyle? No, not today. And, by the way," he added, turning toward Howard, "I think I must have spoken rashly about him just now. There is nothing wrong in his make-up; he may appear queer, but he's all right when you come down to principle. He thinks the world of you."

"I don't want him to think anything of me."

Bodney did not stay to reply. His fever was now so strong that it would have taken two giants to hold him. He fought his way through the crowd, and, panting, rushed into the poker room. They greeted him with the complimentary encouragement usually poured out upon the arrival of the "sucker." "He'll make you look at your hole card." "Cash my chips." "None of us got any show now." It was nearly dinner time when Bodney sat down to the game, and when the meal was announced he was winner. Goyle came in and sat beside him at the dinner table. "The scheme I spoke to you about is a sure road to fortune," he said, in a low tone.

"Bank robbery?" Bodney asked, smiling with the brightness of a winner.

"No, it's not the robbery of the robbers. It is less dangerous and more profitable—almost legitimate."

"Almost!"

"Yes—but full of sauce."

"Don't you think you'd better tell me what it is?"

"Not now. I want to see you alone—tomorrow. In the meantime make up your mind."

"How can I make up my mind to do something that hasn't been proposed?"

"Make up your mind to agree to my plan no matter what it may be. We are going to ride in carriages."

"Or in a police van, which?" said Bodney, smiling.

Goyle put his hand on Bodney's shoulder. "I see you are in a hurry to get back to the game. All right, but keep your mind on my proposition."

"A proposition that hasn't been made," replied Bodney, getting up from the table. The game was re-forming, for the poker player does not daudle over a meal; he eats just as a pig does—as fast as he can.

It seemed that Bodney's luck had come to stay. "You make your third man every time," said a losing wretch whose rent was past due. A kindlier eye might have seen through him his ragged children, but the eye of the winner looks at his stack—no poverty and no wretchedness softens its glitter.

The offensive fellow was there, sitting to the left

of Bodney, but he was not offensive now; defeat had subdued him; and the Professor was present, in the darkness of hard luck, and with his air of mystery. "You either made your hand or you didn't," he said to a man who had drawn one card.

"You ought to know," the man replied, looking at him with a steady eye. "You are a mind-reader."

"Yes, when there is a mind to read. I will call you." He did so and lost his money.

"You knew what I had in my note," said Bodney. "Don't you remember, when I met you on the corner? You said it was written with a pencil. Why couldn't you tell what that man held—whether or not he had made his flush?"

"Both science and psychology stop and grow dizzy when they come to cards," the Professor replied.

Goyle came in and put his hand on Bodney's shoulder. "Slaughter 'em," he said. "You've got everything coming your way."

"But I don't know how long it will last," Bodney replied.

"Don't scare away your luck with mistrust. And above all, don't forget that I have a proposition to make. Well, I'll see you tomorrow. He went out, humming a tune. Bodney looked round to see whether he was gone, and seemed to be relieved upon seeing him pass out. Now it was time to quit, the slave thought. He had not counted his chips, for that was bad luck, but he must have won nearly sixty dollars. Still the cards kept coming, two pairs holding good, and to quit was an insult to the goddess of good fortune. He remembered hearing a gambler say, speaking of an unlucky player: "He stays to lose, but not to win." At ten o'clock he felt that he had reached his limit, and counted his chips—eighty-seven dollars. "I'll have to quit you," he said, shoving back. And now how bright and spirited the streets were. He threw a piece of silver upon the banner of the salvationists.

CHAPTER XV.

DID NOT TOUCH HER.

As Howard was going out he met Bradley coming up the stairs. "I have caught you in time," said the preacher. "I want you to go to dinner with me—at a place off Van Buren Street, where they cater to the poor."

"It is rather a tough neighborhood for a dinner," Howard replied. "Wouldn't you rather go to a better place?"

"No, I would rather like to see how the unfortunate dine."

They went to a restaurant that opened into an alley. The long room was furnished with plain tables, without cloths, and not clean. There was sand on the floor, and on the whitewashed walls, together with Scriptural texts, against one of which some brute had thrown a quid of tobacco, were placards which read, "Lodging ten cents." They took seats at a table and a girl came up and put down a piece of paper, scrawled upon with a pencil. It was a bill of fare. The price set opposite each dish was five cents, and at the bottom it was announced that any order included bread. The place was gradually filling up with a mottled crowd, negroes, a sprinkle of Chinamen, Greeks, Polish Jews, tramps—and off in a corner sat an American Indian. "The air is bad," said the preacher.

"No worse than the bill of fare," Howard replied. "Let us get out. Don't you see how they are eyeing us?"

"Let us at least make a pretense of eating. I like to watch these odd pieces of driftwood."

"Washed from the wreck of humanity," said Howard.

The preacher looked at him with a sad smile. "Yes, and perhaps not all of them are responsible for the wreck. They couldn't weather the storm."

The crowd was noisy and profane. The preacher spoke to a waitress, a girl with a hard, unconcerned face. "I thought that this place was under the auspices of the gospel," said he.

She did not look at him as she replied: "I believe some sort of a church duck did start it, but a feller named Smith runs it now."

"Then services are not held here."

She looked at him. "What sort of services?"

"Church services."

"Well, I guess not. These guys don't want services—they want grub."

"I believe I will address them," the preacher said to Howard.

"On the subject of foreign missions?" Howard asked.

"A merited sarcasm," the minister replied. "Let us go."

In the alley near the door a woman and a ruffian were quarreling. The woman held a piece of money in her hand and the ruffian was trying to take it from her. A policeman passed down the alley, but paid no attention. The ruffian demanded the money. The woman refused. He knocked her down, took it from her hand and was walking off when Bradley touched him on the shoulder. "Give her back that money," he said. The man drew back his ponderous fist. At that moment Howard ran up. The ruffian looked at him and let his arm fall. Bradley called the policeman. He turned and came walking slowly back, swinging his club. "What's wanted?" he asked. Bradley told him what had occurred. "It's a lie!" exclaimed the woman, stepping forward. "You never hit me, did you, Jack?"

"Never touched her," said Jack, and a group about the door of the restaurant roared with laughter. "Move on," said the policeman, and Howard and the preacher moved on, the crowd jeering them.

"What put it into your head to go there?" Howard asked.

"I thought it was my duty."

"A man's duty lies mostly among his own people," said the young lawyer.

"No, among stricken humanity."

"A heroic idea, but fallacious. The Lord takes care of His own. These people are evidently not His own. Pardon my slang, but here is a genuine gospel shop. Let us go in."

At the door of a room forbiddingly neat to the class which it intended to feed, they were met by a cool young woman and a ministerial man. It was a coffee house established to offset the influence of the saloon. At the rear end of the room a young fellow played upon a wheezing melodion. Girls were serving coffee. On the walls were pictures of the Prodigal's Return, Daniel in the Lion's Den, Jacob before Pharaoh, The Old Home, several cows, a horse with his head over a barred gate, and a child lamenting over a broken doll. Howard called attention to the fact that the sandwiches were thin and that the coffee looked pale. "It is charity," said he, "and charity is pale. Now, let me take you to the enemy—the den against which these mild batters are directed."

They went to a saloon. The place was ablaze with light. The walls were hung with paintings, some of them costly, some modest, others representing figures as nude as Lorado's nymphs. On a side counter was a roast of beef, weighing at least a hundred pounds. "Look at that," said Howard. "Vice sets us a great roast—and for five cents, a glass of beer, the vagabond may feast."

"The devil pandering to the drunkard and the glutton," replied the preacher.

"But the devil is not pale; he is not niggardly—he is bountiful. To cope with him, Virtue must be more liberal—give more beef and better coffee."

"Good," said the minister. "I am going to preach a sermon on the Virtue of Vice."

"Red beef versus pale coffee," Howard said, as they stepped out. "And now," he added, "let us get something to eat and then go home."

"Home," repeated the preacher. "I have no home—I have lodgings.

"I know, and I mean that you must go home with me."

Bradley muttered a protest, but was delighted at the thought of seeing Agnes again so soon. He had spent the afternoon at the Judge's house, had left to unite in marriage a servant girl and a hackman, and now wanted an excuse to return, not that he needed one, for the Judge had urged upon him the freedom of the house; but timid love must show cause, or rather must apologize to appearances. And, though the cause now was not strong, yet he argued that the fact of meeting Howard would make it valid enough. He felt that his secret was not known to the Judge, as if that would have made any difference; and he was sure that the girl did not more than suspect him. He wanted her to suspect him, for there was a sweetness in it, but he wanted it to be as yet only a suspicion. He did not acknowledge that he had quite made up his mind regarding her fitness as a wife; and when a man thus reasons he is hopelessly entangled. When a man decides that a woman is not fitted to be his wife he may have arrived at reason but has stopped short of love.

They went to a place that makes a specialty of crabs and sat down in the cool breath of an electric fan. "Quite a difference in our bill of fare," said Bradley, taking up a long card framed in brass edged wood.

"And quite as much difference in our company," Howard replied.

"The old saying, Howard: 'One half the world doesn't know how the other half lives.'"

"Doesn't know how the other half dies," said Howard.

"You are sententious tonight. I have led you into a place that has sharpened your wits."

"But not into a place that sharpened my appetite. But it makes a meal all the more enjoyable afterward. Do you find anything that hits your fancy?"

During the meal the preacher talked of the vices of a great city. A truthful farmer could have told him that there are almost as many vices in the country, and an observant moralist could have assured him that the great mass of women parading the sidewalks at night were sent thither by the rural reprobate, proprietor of a horse and buggy.

"Vice is in man," said Howard.

"Ah, but how are we to eradicate it?"

"By educating woman."

"I don't know that I fully comprehend you."

"Were you ever in a place where women are shameless?"

"No," said the preacher. "The only shameless women I ever met are those who accost me in the street."

"And if," said Howard, "you were to go into a thousand such places you would not meet a well-educated woman. Some of them are bright; some speak several languages, but I have yet to find one who speaks good English. But we are on a subject that is as old as the ocean. It is, however, always new to one in your profession, I suppose. You preach about it, and innocence wonders at your insight, but the young fellow who reports your sermon laughs in his sleeve."

"But, my gracious, Howard, what must we do, ignore it all?"

"I give it up."

"You are young to take so gloomy a view."

"Oh, I don't view it at all," said Howard. "I shoulder my way through it."

An elderly woman, handsomely dressed, came up and held out her hand to the preacher, who arose, bowed over it and declared his pleasure at meeting her. Then he introduced her to Howard, a woman noted for her work in the slums. A part of her labor was to talk morality to the girls in department stores, to make them pious and virtuous on three dollars a week. She kept a house of refuge which she visited once a day, to talk to the women who had been gathered in from the streets and the dens rented to vice by the rich. Her register showed that within the past ten years thousands of women had been reclaimed. But the register did not show how many had gone back to loud music and shame, preferring the glare of infamy, tired out with the simmer of the tea-kettle and the shadows of the kitchen. The preacher had visited her place and had complimented her upon the work she was doing.

"Oh, what has become of Margaret, the blonde girl?"

The matron shook her head. "She became dissatisfied and left us."

"And the one called Fanny. Where is she?"

"Oh, she was too pretty and went away."

"And Julia?"

"Didn't you hear about her? Well, well. Why, the newspapers were full of it. She left us and shortly afterward married a rich man. He took her to his mansion and gave her everything that heart could wish, but it did not suffice. He returned home after an absence from the city to find a drunken crowd in his house, and he turned her out. I am so glad to have met you again. Good-bye."

Bradley began to talk of something foreign, to lead Howard's mind away, but the young man looked at him with a smile and said: "You see that a palace is not even sufficient.'

"Her moral nature had not been trained," Bradley replied.

"It is not that, Mr. Bradley. Her miserable little head had not been trained. Morality without intellectual force is a weakness waiting for a temptation."

"Don't say that, Howard; it is a monstrous thought. Brain is not the whole force of this life. There is something stronger than brain. Love is stronger."

"Yes, it overturns brain. And I will not argue against it, though it might be the cause of thousands of wretched feet on our thoroughfares tonight. It is a glory or a disgrace. But we have been moralists long enough. Let us go home."

CHAPTER XVI.

WITH AN EAR TURNED TOWARD THE DOOR.

Mrs. Elbridge met Howard and the preacher in the hall. She told them that the girls had gone to a meeting of the Epworth League, a short distance away. They had gone to a religious gathering held in the interest of the young, but the preacher felt a deadening sense of disappointment. "They will be back soon," said Mrs. Elbridge, seeming to divine the effect her information had made upon him. Howard heard his father and Uncle William talking in the office. "We will wait for the girls in here," he said, leading the way into the drawing room. Mrs. Elbridge went in to tell the Judge, and shortly afterward entered the drawing room with him. The old gentleman paid no attention to Howard, but warmly shook hands with Bradley, as if he had not seen him only a few hours before.

"Delighted to see you, Mr. Bradley."

Howard glanced at his mother and she read a

communication in his eye. It was that in the old man's enthusiasm there was added evidence of mental weakness. The Latin may express delight at seeing one a dozen times a day, but with an Anglo-Saxon more than one "delight" within twenty-four hours is an extreme.

Bradley looked embarrassed. He said that he was glad to see the Judge, which was hardly true, as he was not prepared at that moment to be glad or even pleased. His heart had gone over to the Epworth League, not to worship God, but one of God's creatures, which, after all, is a pardonable backsliding. He remarked that he and Howard had encountered quite an adventure, giving it in detail, but to avoid any moralizing, having had enough of that for one evening, hastened to change the subject, asking if Mr. William had become any nearer settled as to his dates. This brought a flow of good humor. The Judge looked toward the door. "He has so far improved," said he, "as to admit that at times he may possibly be wrong. I asked him if it were possible to be right, and then we had our battle to fight over again." He offered the preacher a cigar, but ignored his son. The mother noticed it and sighed. Howard smiled at her sadly, and shook his head. Bradley took the cigar abstractedly and after holding it for a time, offered it to Howard, who declined it. The Judge glanced at him but said nothing. William came in. "John," said he, after speaking to Bradley, "I saw old Bodsford this morning."

"Not old Bill Bodsford."

"Yes, sir, old Bill."

"I thought he died years ago."

"No, he has been out in Colorado. I haven't seen him since seventy-eight."

"Are you sure?" the Judge asked, winking at Bradley.

"I ought to know. I met him in St. Louis in seventy-eight—seventy-eight or seventy-nine—in July, about the fifth."

"About the fifth. How can a date be about the fifth?"

"I mean that it was either the fourth, fifth or sixth. He told me then that he was on his way to New Orleans, by boat. It was during that intensely hot weather when so many people were sun—but that was in seventy-nine, wasn't it?"

"I don't remember," said the Judge, winking at Howard by mistake and then frowning to undeceive him.

"Yes, I think it was."

"Seventy-nine," said the preacher, at a venture.

"Then I couldn't have seen old Bill in seventy-eight. But I saw him today—and he looks like a grizzly bear. And he didn't seem to be in very good circumstances. But the last time I saw him before that—"

"In seventy-nine," interrupted the Judge.

"Well, I'm not so sure about that, John. Let me see. I was in St. Paul and went from there directly to St. Louis. Yes. Now, I haven't been in St. Paul but once since seventy-eight and that was year before last. Went directly to St. Louis. It must have been seventy-eight, John. Yes, it was."

"Well, go ahead with your story," said the Judge.

"Oh, it's no story. I was simply telling you when I met old Bill the last time."

"And is that all there is to it?"

"All! Isn't it enough? I didn't start to tell a story and you know it well enough. Look here, Howard," he added, turning upon the young lawyer, "are you fixing to jump on me, too?"

"Not at all, Uncle Billy."

"Oh, Uncle Billy, is it? Then I know you've got it in for me. Mr. Bradley, I studied for the ministry—not very hard, I admit—but I studied, and I am sorry sometimes that I didn't go so far as to put on the cloth. It would have at least protected me from ridicule."

Bradley smiled upon him in a lonesome sort of way, with his ear turned toward the front door, listening for the coming of Agnes. The family joke, so eternally green for the Judge, was but dry grass to him. His soul was panting for the sweet waters of love, the babbling brook of a girl's delightful mischief. But the mind can talk shop while the soul is panting. "You no doubt would have added strength to our profession," he said. "I call it profession in want at the present moment of a better term. Why did you give up your intention? Not want of faith, I hope."

Mrs. Elbridge shook her head as if to imply that there could be no want of faith in one connected with her family. "Well, I don't know," said William. "But the scheme, if I may so express it, struck me as being not exactly useless, but, let us say, hopeless."

"Hopeless," echoed the preacher.

"Yes. The warfare has been going on nearly two thousand years, and the victory is not yet in sight."

"At what date did it begin?" the Judge asked.

William began to puff up. "Now, look here,

John, this is a serious discussion. Is it possible that there is nothing serious except in the law, in the names of your old clients? Do you keep everything serious shut up in your safe?"

The Judge's countenance changed, like the sudden turning down of a light, and he made a distressful gesture. "Don't, William; don't say that."

"Why, what did I say to shock you so?"

The Judge got up and slowly walked back into his office. William looked at Mrs. Elbridge. "Rachel, did I say anything?"

"He isn't well, William, and we never know what is going to displease him. But he means nothing by it, Mr. Bradley," she added. "Sometimes he begins to joke in its old way, but it has been long since we heard his laugh in its old heartiness. I wish you would talk to him, Mr. Bradley. I know he is not well, but he won't permit a doctor to come near him."

The preacher assured her that he would. He did not believe that there was any serious trouble; it was the strain of former years now claiming its debt of his constitution. "Nature does not forget," said he. "But nature may be humored. I have noticed a change in him, but I am inclined to think that he is gradually improving."

Howard was silent, though the minister looked at him at the conclusion of his speech as if expecting some sort of reply. "He doesn't forget about my dates, no matter how much of a change he has undergone," said William. "But, as to our discussion: I read some little in those days, and my mind led me into bogs and swamps—into doubts, if I may say so. It seemed to me that the whole plan was marked out and couldn't be changed. I remember having come across this startling question: 'If man can make his own destiny; if he can, by his own free will, arrest the accomplishment of the general plan, what becomes of God?' That struck me, sir, like a knockout blow."

"And yet," said Howard, "you say that the French have a slop which they call literature."

"What! I said so? Well, what if I did?"

"You have quoted Balzac."

"Have I? But, sir, do you appoint yourself to preside over my conscience?"

"I didn't say anything about your conscience, Uncle Billy."

"Oh, no, but you Uncle Billy me into a broil, that's what you do."

The preacher's mind had caught the quotation, relating as it did to the shop, and he smiled as he said: "I am afraid, Uncle William, that the young man has read too much for us. In an argument he is a porcupine with sharp quills."

"A pig with the bristles of impudence," said William, and smiled an apology to the mother.

"Nevertheless," remarked the preacher, returning to the subject, "I don't see how the eye of faith could have been dimmed by such a mote. Conscience—"

"Meaning education," Howard interrupted.

The minister bowed to Howard, but continued to address himself to William. "Conscience ought to have pointed out the good you could do. You could at least have gone to a foreign country—"

"Or off Van Buren Street," said Howard.

Bradley braced himself for a debate. Alone with Howard he might have said, "let it pass," but in the presence of a woman, a believer in his faith, a preacher must not shun a controversy. It would be an acknowledgment of the strength of the doubt and of the weakness of faith. So he braced himself against the wall of creed, and with polemic finger raised was about to proceed when he heard the front door open.

"The girls," said Mrs. Elbridge, glad enough to break in.

"So soon?" remarked Bradley, looking at his watch and meaning so late. Florence and Agnes came in, laughing. Bradley got up with a bow. "You here?" said Agnes, and then corrected herself by saying that she was pleased to see him there. "I never know how anything is going to sound," she continued, throwing her hat on a sofa. "It's all improvisation with me. I never saw as awkward a man in my life—" Bradley looked at her with such a start that she hastened to exclaim: "Oh, not you, Mr. Bradley—the young man who walked home with us. I couldn't for the life of me get it out of my head that he wasn't on stilts." She sat down on the sofa. Bradley made bold to go over and sit down beside her, taking up her hat, looking about for some place to put it and ending by holding it on his knees, awkwardly pressing them together. He felt that Howard was laughing at him; he knew that Agnes was. But she didn't offer to take the hat. Florence, however, relieved him, and then everyone laughed except William. The preacher had been placed in an awkward position, though anyone might have made a grace of it—anyone but a man whom custom almost forces to adopt solemnity as a badge of office; and William gave Howard credit for it all. In certain humors he would have charged the young man with a rainy day, a frost or a cold wind. He looked at him in his reproachful way and cleared his throat.

"What is it now, Uncle William?" Howard asked.

"Oh, don't ask me. You ought to know."

"But I don't. I haven't said a word or done a thing that you should give me the bad eye."

"Rachel," said the old man, "it seems to me that the more he reads the more slang he uses. The 'bad eye!' That belongs to the police court."

"Then it is not a quotation from Balzac."

"Never you mind about quotations. I have quoted before you were born—and I knew, sir, from what source. But I won't stay to be browbeaten. I will leave you."

"By the way," Howard called after him, "if you want a pipe of good tobacco step into my room. You'll find a fresh can on the table."

"I don't want any of your tobacco, sir; I don't want anything you've got."

Bradley might have thought that in this family the joke was overworked, that is, had he been prepared to think anything. But he was not. His mind was aglow from the light beside him, and his ideas, if at that moment he had any, were as gold fishes in a globe, swimming round and round.

Florence went to the piano. Howard stood beside her. Mrs. Elbridge went out. It was time, and she knew it. William appeared at the door. "I thought you said that your tobacco was on the table in your room. What right have you got—what cause have I ever given you to deceive me in that way?"

"You said you didn't want any of my tobacco."

"You said it was on the table. Of course I don't want it—I wouldn't have it."

"You just wanted to see where it was."

"I don't care anything about it, sir. I want you to understand that as you go along."

"All right, but the can of tobacco, I remember now, is in the closet on the shelf."

William went away, and the young man knew that in the morning his tobacco can would be empty. Florence played the air of a slow, old love song, and between the notes fell the soft words, her own and Howard's; they looked into each other's eyes, eyes so familiar to both, eyes they could no more remember first seeing than we can remember the first sky, the first star—love as old as recollection and as young as the moment.

There is one thing we can always say, and Bradley said it: "I shall miss you when you are gone."

"I'm not gone yet," Agnes replied.

"I hope you are not getting tired of us."

"Tired?" She raised her eyes and he looked into them, into the depth of their blue mystery. "No, I am having lots of fun."

"Fun! Is that all?"

"Isn't that enough? That's all I want."

"But life is not all fun."

"No?" She raised her eyes again.

"Life is serious," he said. "The greatest joy is serious; the greatest happiness comes to the heart when the heart is solemn."

"Oh, I don't think so. I cry when I'm serious."

"There is joy in a tear."

"Not in mine."

He did not hear the front door open. For him all the world had come in. He did not hear a step at the door. Bodney came in. Florence left off playing and turned about on the stool. Bradley arose and shook hands with him, said that he was glad to meet him, and lied. He would not at that moment have been glad to see the glory promised to the faithful. But he lied, as we all of us are compelled to lie, for to lie at times is the necessary martyrdom of the conscience. Bodney's face was bright and his laugh was gay. "You are as merry as a serenade," said Florence.

"As happy as a lark," he replied. The love-making was spoiled. Bradley said that it was time to take his leave. Bodney followed him to the door, and beneath the hall light handed him a bank note, apologizing for not having sooner returned the loan of ten dollars.

"But you have given me twenty," said Bradley.

"Have I? Then give the extra ten to the church."

CHAPTER XVII.

LYING ON THE SIDEWALK.

Bradley lived in Aldine Square. By the light of the first gas lamp he looked at his watch and found that it wanted but three minutes to midnight. At the corner of the street he waited for a cross-town car, but as none was within sight, he walked on, thinking little of the distance home, which was not great, for his mind was on Agnes. He had not decided that she would make a good wife, but he knew that he would ask her to marry him. He believed that his happiness depended upon her decision. This is a conclusion reached by nearly every man. His salary was not large, for his church was poor, but it was growing rich in numbers and that meant a popularity insuring larger pay. But why should he consider his income? They could live happily in Aldine Square. It was a charming place, and so romantic that one would scarcely expect to find it in Chicago. It might have been a part of Paris. It was come upon suddenly, its gate,

LYING ON THE SIDEWALK.   205

with two great posts of stone, opening into the street. There was a plastered wall, and it looked as if it had been built for ages. Through the gate, which was always left open, the view was attractive—there were trees, shrubbery, flowers, a pool, a fountain and a carriage drive. It would charm Agnes.

The street was deserted, with the exception of a straggler here and there, turned out of a saloon. "Vice shutting its red eye," he mused, as one place closed its door. Looking ahead he saw a man leaning against a lamp post. As Bradley came up the man, stepping out, said: "Mister, will you please tell me what time it is?"

Bradley halted and took out his watch, and, holding it so as to catch the light, was about to tell him when the man snatched the watch, broke the chain and fled down an alley. The preacher shouted after him, ran a short distance down the alley, but, realizing that pursuit was folly, if not dangerous, returned to the street and continued his way homeward, the piece of chain dangling from his pocket. He thought of going to the nearest station to report the robbery, but his mind flew back to Agnes. How delicious it would be to have her all to himself, sitting by the fountain in the summer air. The perfume of the flowers would be sweeter, the falling of the water more musical. They would read together till the twilight came, read silly books, if she preferred them; and in the twilight they would read a book in which God had written—the book of their own hearts. And in cold weather they would sit in the warm light, at the window, and look out upon the little park, the shrubbery covered with snow, the statuary of winter. He would never seek to change the current of her mind. Nature had fashioned it a laughing rivulet and it should never be a sighing wave. With her in the congregation he could be more eloquent, touch more hearts through his love for her; he would be more akin to the young, for her love would be as a stream of youth constantly flowing into his life. Nature might have shown her power in the creation of man, but surely her glory in the creation of woman. He drew a contrast between Florence and Agnes. Florence was stronger, and had more dignity; but, of course, he believed that Agnes was more affectionate, and love was more beautiful than strength.

He turned into the street leading to the Aldine gate. And how quiet everything was. It was a love night, the leaves murmuring. But, what was that lying on the sidewalk in front of the gate? A woman. He stood looking down at her. Could she have been murdered. The light was not strong, but he could see that she was not ill dressed. She was lying on her right side. He touched her shoulder and she turned upon her back with a moan. He leaned over her and caught the fumes of liquor. But he got down upon his knees, raised her head and spoke to her.

"What are you doing here, poor girl?" he said. The light falling upon her face showed that she was young. She moaned and mumbled something. He asked her where she lived, but she could not tell him.

"I don't know what to do with you," he said.

"Don't leave me," she mumbled.

"I will be back in a moment," he said, placing her with her back against the wall. Then he ran to the fountain, wet his handkerchief, and returning with it dripping, bathed her face. It was hot and feverish. The cold handkerchief appeared somewhat to revive her.

"Don't you know where you live?"

"I can't—don't know the number."

"Nor the street?"

"Nothing."

Again he bathed her face, and taking his hat fanned her with it. "How did you come here?"

"They must have left me."

"Then you were with someone."

"Yes—three."

"Where had you been?"

"Wine room. Don't turn me over to the police. I won't go there again."

"Can't you remember now where you live?"

"It is a long ways from here—over on the West Side. I won't go there in this fix. I would rather die."

"Then I don't know what to do."

"Don't turn me over to the police," she moaned.

He stood with his hat in his hand, looking up and down the street. From the corner came the whack of the policeman's club against a lamp post. Not far away the fountain splashed its music. "Can you walk?" he asked.

"I'll try. But where are you going to take me?"

"To my home."

"No," she cried piteously. "I don't want a woman to see me this way."

"No woman is there to see you. Come on."

He led her along, supporting her with his arm. He did not look to see if there were any windows lighted about the square; he did not think of scandal; he thought of the poor thing heavy upon his arm, not as a preacher, but as a man. He carried her up the stone steps, unlocked the door and went into the hall, into the red light falling from the lamp. Up the stairs he led her, into a front room, striking a match as he entered, lighted the gas and eased her down upon a chair. She was deathly pale.

"Let me lie down," she said.

He pointed to the bed, stepped out into another room and drew the portieres. Then he lay down upon a sofa, not to think of what he had done, but of Agnes.

He was awakened by the housekeeper's tap upon the door. "Come in," he called, and as she entered he thought of the woman. The housekeeper was fat and full of scandal. She walked straightway to the portieres and drew them aside to enter the room, and started back with a gasp of surprise.

"My sister," said Bradley. "She came on a late train, and is going out early. Don't disturb her. She brought me bad news from home, and must go on further to see my other brother. She could not explain by telegraph. It involves the settling of an estate."

He was now standing beside the housekeeper and could see into the adjoining room. The girl, with a remnant of modesty, had drawn the covering over her.

Two days later, Sunday, at the close of services, a woman came forward, held out her hand to Bradley and said: "I want you to pray for me."

Her face was pale and there was true repentance in her eyes. "You are my sister," Bradley replied, and this time he did not believe that he had told a falsehood. She went out, with tears on her cheeks; and a lady who had come up to compliment the preacher on his sermon, asked:

"Who is that girl?"

"I don't know her name."

"She met me just as I was coming in," said the lady, and was anxious as to whether or not this was your church. She was evidently not looking for denominations."

She was not. She was looking for something nearer God—a man.

CHAPTER XVIII.

MADE HIS PROPOSITION.

The farmers have a saying to illustrate restlessness: "Like a hen on a hot griddle." And Bodney thought of it the next day, as he sat about the office waiting for the noon hour, for the game did not start before then. He tried to read, but the words were as the echo of a pot that had been played. He attempted to write, but called it a misdeal. How swift was life, viewed from the window, and yet how slow time was, limping, halting, standing still, boulders between minutes and mountains between hours. Surely his watch was slow. No, for a bell confirmed it in its record of the forenoon's slothfulness. He thought of Goyle, and wondered why he did not come to make his proposition, if it were so important. He went out to walk in the cool air blowing from the lake, and the Wexton stairs arose before him. He rang the bell, and, standing there waiting for the grim face of the porter, reminded himself of an old horse at a stable door. Inside they were cleaning up, sweeping, dusting, getting ready for another day and another night. From off in a bedroom came the snoring of a man who had gone to sleep, drunk and broke; but the porter would bid him a pleasant good-morning and would give him a drink from a bottle kept in ice all night. Bodney sat down at a window and took up a newspaper and glanced at the report of a committee appointed to investigate gambling in Chicago. Numerous witnesses had been summoned, some of them connected with the poker clubs; and in a vague way they admitted under oath that they might have seen men playing cards for money, but could not recall exactly where. "I am looking for a fool," said the Legislature. "What do you want with him?" the Governor asked. "I want to put him on an investigative committee," the Legislature replied. "For the city?" the Governor inquired. "Yes," answered the Legislature. "Then," said the Governor, "take the first countryman you come to."

Men with borrowed money burning in their pockets began to arrive, and each one was asked by an earlier comer if he wanted to play poker, and though he had shouldered his way through the crowd to get there, fearing that he might not find a vacant seat, he answered in a hesitating way, "Well, I don't know; haven't got much time—might play a little while." It was a part of the hypocrisy of the game, recognized by all and practiced by all.

The noon meal was munched and the game began. Opposite Bodney sat a man whose liquor lapped over from the previous day. One eye was smaller than the other, and on one cheek, red and flaming, was a white scar. He drew to everything, won from the start and was therefore offensive. Bodney opened a pot on a pair of aces. All passed but the man with the white scar, who said that he would stay. "You are a pretty good fellow," he remarked to Bodney. "I'll help you along." Bodney drew three cards and caught his third ace. The white scar drew two cards. Bodney, to lead him on, bet a chip.

"Well," said the scar, "I had a pair of sixes and an ace here. I'll go down now and see if I helped, and I won't bet you unless I have. Well, I'll have to raise you three dollars."

"Raise you three," said Bodney.

"You must have helped. Still, we never know. Ain't that so, Jim?"

Jim said that it was so, and the scar, as if pleased

and reassured in thus finding his view confirmed, raised Bodney.

It was wrong to take a drunken man's money; it was robbery, but it was poker, and Bodney raised him.

"Well, you play two pairs pretty hard, and I don't believe you can beat three sixes. Raise you." Then Bodney began to study. "I'll call you," he said.

"I drew to three little diamonds," said the fellow, "and caught a flush." He spread his hand. Bodney swore. "I never played with a drunken man that he didn't beat me."

The fellow looked up at him as he raked in the pot. "Have to do it. My pew rent's due. Ain't that right, Jim?"

"That's right," said Jim.

Bad ran into worse and rounded up in a heap of disaster. At three o'clock, just as the game was getting good, as someone remarked, Bodney went out, feeling in his pockets. This becomes a habit with the poker fool. He continues to search himself long after he has raked up the lint from the bottom of his pockets. In the street the air was stagnant and the sunshine was a mockery. At several places he tried to borrow money, but failed;

his former accommodater, the druggist, told him that he had a note to meet and could not spare it. He was sorry, he said. Bodney went out, muttering that he was a liar. He went to the office and found the door locked. Howard was not there, and he could hide himself, the peacock whose tail feathers had been pulled out. But before going into the office he thought of the old doctor across the hall, and hesitated. Perhaps he had money, and, having ruined his mind, might be fool enough to lend it. The doctor was pleased to see him. He was astonished to find Bodney so much interested in his affairs, and he wondered if a spirit of reformation had come upon the youth of the land. Bodney said that of late he had begun to hear much of the old man's skill as a physician. The old man turned a whitish smile upon him and listened like a gray rat, bristles resembling feelers sticking out on his lip. And after a time Bodney asked if he would be so kind as to lend ten dollars till the following morning? He was sorry, but could not. That part of the mind which takes account of money is the last to suffer from disease.

Bodney went into the office to wait for something, he did not know what. He thought of Bradley, and wondered if he could find him. Just then he discovered the something he had been waiting for. Goyle came in.

"Halloa, old man," said Goyle. "I went up to the club just now to look for you and they told me that you had gone down stairs."

"Down stairs broke," Bodney replied.

"That's all right," said Goyle.

"It's not all right. I'm broke, I tell you; and a man that's broke is all wrong."

"He may think so. I'm glad you are broke." He put his hand on a table, leaned forward, and gazed into Bodney's eyes.

"Glad," said Bodney, blinking.

"Yes, glad. It teaches you the need of money. You are forced to shove back your chair, to give your place to a brute standing behind you. You see the deal go on. You are frozen out, but no one cares. That game is life, the affairs of man epitomized; you put in your last chip, you lose, and you have failed in business. A fellow who hasn't one-tenth the education has succeeded. He stacks up the chips that you have bought, and for consolation he says that chips have no home. Am I right?"

"Yes, you are. But I want to get back into the affairs of man. Let me have ten dollars."

"Two weeks from now I can give you ten thousand. Listen to me. Wait a moment." He closed the door, came back, drew a chair in front of Bodney, sat down and leaned forward. "Now, I will submit my proposition."

"I don't know that I can entertain any proposition. I am in too desperate a fix to go into any sort of an enterprise. My blood is full of fever. I've got this gambling mania on me and I'm tempted to cut my throat. One evening you took me to a supper that was not to cost anything. It has cost everything, all the money I had, my honor, my future, my—"

"That's rot, George. I introduced you to a supper that gave you experience—real knowledge of the world. You have met men without their dresscoats—you know man as he is and not as he says he is. You were blind and I opened your eyes to the fact that money is not the reward of the honest and industrious. It is the agent of hell, and must be won by means of the devil. You ought to have been a rich man. If there'd been any foresight you would have been. And whose fault was it that the opportunity slipped? Not yours. Now to my plan. Look at me. Child stealing."

"What!" Bodney exclaimed.

"I have laid my wires. We will steal children

and gather in thousands of dollars in reward for restoring them to their parents. Hold on. Look at me. We will steal from the rich, for that is always legitimate. We will have our agents stationed here and there—we will—"

"Infamous scoundrel, I could cut your throat. I wish to God I had."

"Sit down and listen to me."

"I won't sit down. I will stand and look you in the eye, you scoundrel. Don't put your hand on me. Stand back, or I'll knock you down."

Goyle sneered at him. "You can't hit me. I am your master. Now, listen to me. I am going over into Michigan to establish a—post, I'll call it. And when I come back, you will join me. I present a plan by which you can get out of all your difficulties, and you turn on me. Is that the way to treat a benefactor? I have settled upon our first enterprise. Every day a nurse and child are at a certain place in Lincoln Park. The father is dead and the mother is rich. The child, I have found from the nurse, is a boy. I am engaged to marry her. While I am walking with her you steal—"

Bodney struck him in the mouth—struck him with all the force of disgrace and dispair. He fell and the blood flowed from his mouth. He did not

Bodney struck him in the mouth.

get up; he lay with his head back, and Bodney thought that he saw death in his half-closed eyes. He touched him with his foot and spoke to him, but he did not move. Someone knocked at the door, and without a tremor Bodney opened it, expecting to find Howard. The old doctor stood in the hall. "I am sorry I refused to let you have the money," he said. "And now, if you assure me that—"

"I am obliged to you," Bodney broke in, "but I do not need it. I wanted to gamble with it, but I have quit gambling. I have overthrown the evil. Here," he added, taking the old man's arm and leading him into the room. "There it lies bleeding," he said, pointing. "Perhaps it needs your assistance. I must bid you good day." He walked out, leaving the old man alone with Goyle.

"What are you smiling at?" asked an acquaintance who met him in the street.

"Was I smiling?"

"Yes, like a four-time winner."

"I am at least a one-time winner," Bodney replied. He stepped into a drug store to get a cold drink, his friend's place, he noticed after entering. The druggist came forward and thus spoke to him: "I was sorry after you went out that I didn't let you have ten dollars. I found that I had more than enough to meet the note. I can let you have it now."

Bodney shook his head. "No, I thank you—I don't care for it. I have quit borrowing."

"I hope you don't feel offended."

"Not at all. I am grateful to you for not lending it to me."

Late in the evening he went back to the office. No one was there, but soon the negro janitor came in and pointed to a damp spot on the floor. "I have washed up the blood where the man fainted and fell," he said. "The doctor brought him to all right, and there's a note on the table he left for you."

Bodney opened the note and read: "I leave for Michigan, and will be back within a few days. I don't blame you as much as I do myself. I permitted you to break away from me, but you will come back and at last be thankful. Goyle."

CHAPTER XIX.

THE GIRL AGAIN.

Bodney's "breaking away" from Goyle had taken place on the day following the night when Bradley had been robbed of his watch, and two days before the girl appeared in church to ask for prayers. On the Monday following, about noon, she appeared again, this time at Bradley's lodgings. The housekeeper answered her ring at the bell. "Ah," she said, "come in. You are Mr. Bradley's sister, I believe. I didn't see you but a moment, but I think I recognize you."

"Is Mr. Bradley here?" the girl asked.

"No, your brother has gone out. I think you can find him over at Judge Elbridge's. I don't know exactly where it is, but some place on Indiana Avenue. Anyone can tell you. I hope you haven't any more bad news for him."

The girl was shrewd and did not betray herself. "No," she said, and went away. Bradley was in the Judge's drawing room with Agnes when a servant came in to tell him that a young woman at the door wished to see him.

"Oh, a young woman," cried Agnes, pretending to pout. "Some girl you have been talking sweet to, I warrant." He had risen to go out, but he halted to lean over and say to her, "I have never talked sweet, as you term it, to anyone—except—"

"This one," Agnes broke in. "Oh, go on. Don't let me detain you."

"Probably someone connected with the church—"

"Of course, they always are. Go on, please."

"I will tell you all about her when I come back."

"Oh, don't mind me. Here's Florence. She knows I don't care. Do please go on."

Bradley went out, and not with a light heart, for his love had now entered into the stew and fretful state. The girl stood in the hall, and in the dim light he did not recognize her till she spoke. She handed him a small package.

"What is this?" he asked.

"It is yours."

"My what?"

"Your watch."

It was some time before he could speak. All ideas were as dust blown about his mind. "You don't mean to say that—you couldn't have taken it—you—"

"Let me go where I can talk to you—outside."

He went out with her and together they walked along the street. Looking back, he saw Agnes at the window, and he waved his hand at her. She made a face at him, he thought. "Now, what is it you have to say?"

"You know a man named Goyle?" she said.

"Yes, I have met him at the Judge's house."

He waited for her to proceed. "I was with him and two others the night you found me. They left me on the sidewalk because I could not go further, I have been told. Goyle went away alone and snatched your watch."

"But, my gracious, how do you know? Did he tell you?"

"For some time he has been coming to see me. He was the first man I ever went with to—a place where I should not have gone. I blush to own it, but I was fascinated by him. He asked me to marry him, and I consented. The last time he came after that night was yesterday evening. But you had taught me to despise him. I could not drive him away, however, so I sat in the room with him. His mouth had been hurt—two of his teeth were gone. He said he had fallen off a car. He said also that as soon as he got a little better he was going to Michigan. He took out his watch, one that I had never seen him have before, and I noticed that it had a broken chain. Then I remembered seeing a broken chain hanging from your pocket; and the next morning before I left your house I thought I heard you tell someone that your watch had been snatched from you. I asked him to let me see the watch, and in it I found your name. I did not return it to him—I jumped up and ran out. He called after me, and tried to catch me, but I slammed a door in his face and locked it. Then, my mother, who never did like him, ordered him out of the house."

"What is your name?"

"Margaret Frayer."

"Then, Margaret Frayer, I am sorry you brought me the watch."

"Sorry?"

"I did not wish a reward for what I had done for you."

"Oh, that—the watch is not your reward. You have saved a soul. In my heart I believe that I have found peace. I went to sleep with a prayer on my lips, and I awoke with such a joy in my heart that I was frightened. I called mother and she came running into the room, and there must have been a spirit there, for before I said a word, and before mother had seen me, for it was dark, she cried out that I was saved. She had always been worried over me; she feared that my soul was lost. And she put her arms about me and sobbed in her happiness. That is your reward, Mr. Bradley."

"Come back to the house with me," he said.

He led her into the drawing room and introduced her to Florence and Agnes. "I wish to present a young woman whom God has smiled upon," he said, and they looked at him in astonishment. He told them that he had found her wandering and had led her home. Florence took her hand.

"I may not be worthy, yet," said Margaret Frayer. "You don't know me well enough to take my hand."

"I know that you must have suffered, and that is enough," Florence replied. The preacher looked at Agnes. He wondered why she did not come oftener to his church. He wondered what she would say to the young woman.

"You are my sister," said Agnes, as if inspired, and Bradley clasped his hands and pressed them to his bosom. His heart was full.

Margaret Frayer did not remain long. "You may meet me again," she said.

"She is to become a member of my church," Bradley spoke up.

"My heart and my prayers will be with your church, Mr. Bradley," she said; "I shall remember you and be grateful to you as long as I live, but my soul tells me to go with the Salvation Army, among girls, and persuade them to work in the street when they have the time. It is not goodness alone that saves us, Mr. Bradley; goodness may be selfish—it is saving others that saves us. You know how that is. You have saved others."

"You are right," he said. "Go with the army; you can do more there."

"And, do you say so?" Florence cried. "I thought you too orthodox for that."

"Not too orthodox for the truth," he replied, bowing.

"Then," said Florence, "I think more of you than I did. I thought it was your ambition to build up a church, but I find that you have forgotten your creed to save a woman. I am coming oftener to hear you preach."

During this time Margaret Frayer stood near the door, waiting, it seemed, for an opportunity to go.

The preacher looked at her, and mused upon the change that had come over her face since he had first seen her, only a short time, but a great change. The Salvation Army has a countenance and a complexion peculiarly its own, serene and pale; and so quick, it seems, is the transformation that the coarse-featured, evil-eyed woman of today may, tomorrow, have a striking refinement. "I hope you will come frequently to my church," said Bradley, taking her hand.

"Whenever I am selfish," she replied.

"You young ladies have done yourselves credit," said Bradley, when Margaret Frayer had taken her leave.

"Why so?" said Agnes. "Because we treated her kindly? Did you take us for heathens?"

"Oh, no, but women—women are so slow to forgive."

"Forgive? Why, what has she done? She simply wanted religion, and you have helped her. Oh, she might have done wrong, I don't know. But women are more forgiving now that they have taken more of man's privileges. They may become quite generous after a while." With Agnes it was innocence; with Florence it was knowledge. She divined the history of the girl; and in giving her hand felt that it was to one who had gone astray, who had suffered, and who had turned back.

The Judge came in, to the disappointment of the preacher, who feared that, soon to be followed by William, the old jurist would begin anew to stir up the old straw of family humor. But William did not come, and the Judge was in no mood for joking. He had been brooding, and his brow was dark. "Florence," he said, after exchanging a few words with Bradley, "I wish you would walk out with me." She said nothing, but went out and came back with her hat. They walked in the shade of the elms, and he remarked upon different objects, but she said nothing.

"Why don't you talk, Florence?"

"Because I haven't anything to say."

"You mean that you have nothing to say to me."

"I mean that it is useless to say anything to you. Shall I say something? I will. You are an unnatural father."

"No, I have an unnatural son."

"That is not true, Judge. Anyone to see him, to hear him talk, to know him, would feel that he could not commit such a crime. Why, sometimes when I am alone it almost exasperates me to think about it; and to realize that I am in a conspiracy against him. It is cruel, and at times I fancy that I am almost as unnatural as you are."

"To be bound by an oath? Is that unnatural? Is it unnatural to have honor? I told you in the first place to protect you; I bound you by oath to protect her, his mother. That is simple enough."

"But you don't know how near I have come to the violation of that oath. More than once I have had it in my heart to tell him—but I couldn't," she broke off. "I couldn't. But he is going away, and I will write it to him, every detail of it; and I know that he will forgive me."

"You make me the criminal when I am the injured. Let us go back."

CHAPTER XX.

THE PREACHER CONFESSES.

Bradley had argued with himself that at the proper time it would be simple enough to tell the girl that he loved her, and no doubt he was right, but the time did not come. He sat beside her on the sofa, when the Judge and Florence had quitted the room, and he looked into her eyes, and the proper words arose like a graceful flight of birds, rich in bright feathers, but they scattered and flew away. He could have delivered an oration upon beauty and love, and he did; but he feared to surprise her by telling her that he loved her. He did not dream that she had discovered it coming before he felt it. It was not possible for so innocent a creature to know so much. He was a large man, and large men may have sentiment, but sometimes they lack sentimental nerve.

"You don't believe now that I talked what you termed sweet to that poor girl, do you?"

"Oh, I don't know. But I don't see why she

should look at you that way even if you did—did lead her. It must have looked nice, you going along leading her. What do you suppose people thought?"

"No one—one saw me lead her," Bradley stammered.

"Oh, then it was in the dark. Led her in the dark."

"She didn't mean that I really took her by the hand and led her. I led her spiritually."

"Is that all? Where did you find her—spiritually?"

"Going—shall I say?"

"Why, of course."

"Going to the devil."

"Oh, and did she say so, or could you see for yourself?"

"I could see. Agnes—Miss Agnes, if I were not afraid of lowering myself in your esteem, I would tell you something."

"Don't tell me anything dreadful," she cried, stopping her ears. "I know it must be something awful."

He waited for her to unstop her ears, which she did very soon, and then he spoke, but on another subject. She replied listlessly, leaning her head on the back of the sofa. He told her about his church and she yawned. He had been delighted to see her in the congregation, and she yawned again. "I thought you were going to tell me about that woman," she said.

"But you stopped your ears."

"And don't you know that when a woman stops her ears it's the time when she wants to hear?"

"I didn't know that."

"You didn't? Then you needn't tell me anything."

"Yes, I believe I ought to tell you—only you."

"Why only me?" she asked, her eyes half closed.

"I don't know, but—"

"Then, why did you say only me?"

"Because I—I think more of you than of anyone else."

"Oh, if you think it's your duty you'd better tell me."

He told her, and she sat up straight, looking at him; she got up and walked slowly to the opposite side of the room, he gazing at her. He reproached himself for telling her. She was young, lived apart from the great crowd, and could not understand. He could not see her face, for she stood with her back toward him, but displeasure has many countenances, and he could see that his story had offended her. Her head was slightly bowed, and she was no doubt weeping; he heard her sob. Then she had loved him, and her love was dying. But he did not dare to go to her, to the death of the love he had murdered. Suddenly she turned about. Her face was radiant, and she was laughing. He stared at her in amazement.

"It is exactly what you ought to have done," she said.

"And I am not lowered in your estimation?"

"For being a truer man than any man I have ever known? Oh, no."

Yes, she had turned round, laughing, but there were tear stains on her cheeks. He did not know that she had passed through a struggle of doubt to reach laughter. Surely she was a strange creature, worthy of being loved and capable of loving; but he did not tell her that he loved her. The words were warm in his heart, but felt cool upon his lips, and he did not utter them. He talked in a roundabout way, in an emotional skirmish, he afterward said to himself, and then took his leave, as the Judge and Florence had returned. Just outside he met Bodney coming in. "Oh, by the way, the very man I want to see, Mr. Bodney. I want a talk with you."

Bodney thought that the preacher was going to thank him again for the money sent to the church, to tell him how much good it had done. "I will walk along with you," he said.

"This is a peculiar world," remarked the preacher, as they strode along, side by side.

"You might almost say a damnable world," Bodney replied.

"No, not quite so bad as that." They walked on in silence, Bodney wondering what the preacher wanted to talk about, the preacher wondering how he could best get at what he intended to say. "You are well acquainted with Mr. Goyle," said Bradley.

"Why do you speak of him? Why didn't you say I am well acquainted with the devil?"

"I suppose I might as well. Do you believe him desperate?"

"In his milder moods, yes; at other times he goes beyond that—he is inhuman."

"Ah. Do you believe that he would snatch a man's watch?"

"He would snatch a woman's child. He is a beast. But you have something to tell me. What is it?"

"I will, but as I do not wish to bring someone else into the glare of scandal, you must keep it to yourself. The other night, as I was going home, a man standing under a lamppost asked me the time. I took out my watch and he snatched it and fled down an alley. I didn't notice his face, or at least I could not see it very well, and I did not recognize him, but I have recovered the watch and have been told that it was Goyle who snatched it. And you do not suppose that there is any question as to his being bold enough to do such a thing."

"Mr. Bradley, that man would do anything; he is a footpad or a sorcerer, just as the humor takes him. Now, I will tell you something. He made himself my master, so completely that at times I could not resist him. But the other day he made me an infamous proposition and I struck him in the mouth and knocked him senseless upon the floor. Blood ran out of his mouth, and it was black —black, I will swear. I left him lying there, and when I returned he was gone, but he had written a note to me, a note in which there was not a word of reproach or resentment. He said he was going away and would see me upon his return. That note frightened me, and I have been scared ever since, dreading to meet him, for I feel that he has some sort of reserve power to throw over me. I would go away, but the thought that he knows all my movements is constantly haunting me. You may smile at this and say that I ought to be stronger, that it is superstition, and that we are not living in a superstitious age, but I tell you that in his presence I feel a weakness come over me to such a degree that when I am with him I have only one strength—a passion for gambling. I have let him ruin me, soul and body; I—"

"I will pray for you," said Bradley.

"You might as well pray for rain, and nothing could be more foolish than that."

"What, you doubt the spirit of God?"

"I believe in the spirit of the devil. But this is jugglery. If he had left me a note full of resentment, or had even left no word at all, I should have felt that I had conquered him; but, as it is, I know that I am his slave."

"My dear young man," said the preacher, "you ascribe to him supernatural powers; you have permitted him to take you back into the middle ages. Such a thing is absurd, in this great, progressive city. See," he added, pointing at an electric car rushing by. "There goes the nineteenth century, and yonder," he broke off, waving his hand at a cart shoved by an Italian, "is the sixteenth century. You have let the Italian put you into his wretched cart. Get out—get on the electric car."

THE PREACHER CONFESSES. 237

"Your illustration is all right, Mr. Bradley; but he has me in his cart bound hand and foot. But we have both said enough, and what we have said is not to be repeated to others. I'll turn back here."

After knocking Goyle down, Bodney had fully determined to make a confession to Howard and the Judge, but upon finding the note his will resolved itself into fear and indecision. He felt, however, that the gambling germ was dead—"germ," he muttered to himself. "Giant!" he cried aloud. It must be, though, that he would gradually gain strength, and the time for the confession was surely not far off. But he would bring disgrace upon himself and be driven out of the house. He could not bear the thought of seeing hatred in the eye of the Judge. The old man was unforgiving; had not forgiven his son, and would surely send Bodney to the penitentiary. "I can't tell him yet," he mused. "I must wait for strength. That scoundrel is thinking of me at this moment, and I know it." In the night he awoke with a feeling that Goyle was in the room, and he sprang out of bed and lighted the gas. Thus it was for three nights, and on the third morning came a letter from Goyle, not a letter, but an envelope directed by his hand, and in it was a newspaper cutting, set in the large type of the village press. "Last night, at Col. Radley's, the guests were entertained in a most novel, not to say startling, manner, by Prof. Goyle, of Chicago, who gave several feats of mind-reading. Miss Sarah Mayhew, daughter of our leading merchant, stuck a pin in the door-facing as high as she could reach, while the Professor was out of the room, and then hid the pin under the carpet. The Professor was brought in blindfolded, amid the silence which the Colonel had enjoined. He took Miss Mayhew by the hand, fell into deep thought for a few moments and then went straightway and took the pin from under the carpet, and then, marvelous to relate, ran across the room and leaping off the floor stuck the pin in the exact hole which it had occupied at the hands of the handsome Miss Mayhew. George Halbin, one of our leading lawyers, said that the feat would have seemed impossible to even a man with both eyes open. The Professor will appear at the opera house tomorrow night, and our citizens who appreciate a good thing when they see it should turn out."

"What have you got there?" William asked, standing in Bodney's door.

THE PREACHER CONFESSES.

"Just a clipping from a newspaper telling of Goyle's wonderful mind-reading."

"Let me see it."

William read the paragraph and handed it back. "I don't believe a word of it," he said. "Those fellows will write anything if they are paid for it. It's all a lie."

"It's all true," said Bodney.

"What, have you turned spiritualist? Is the whole family going to pieces? Howard has ruined himself with French books and John is so snappish that no one can speak to him. Is that the sort of home I've found? Give me that cigar sticking out of your pocket. You don't need it. Thank you. A man who believes the stuff you do don't know whether he's smoking or not. Is that John, roaring at Howard? I want to tell you that there's something wrong here. What do you keep holding that thing for? Why, you shake like a sifter at a sawmill. You are all going crazy."

CHAPTER XXI.

UP THE STAIRS AND DOWN AGAIN.

When Bodney went into the hall he found the Judge walking up and down, waiting for breakfast. His brow was troubled and dark, for Howard had just announced his determination to leave on the following day. He had acknowledged to himself that there was nothing left to hope for, and yet he had continued to hope that it all might be, as Florence believed, a vision, a nightmare, to be relieved by a sudden start. He knew that it was unreasonable thus to hope, but hope was born before reason, and will exist after reason has died of old age. As Bodney approached the old man stood with his hand pressed against his forehead. Bodney's heart smote him, but his fear was stronger than his remorse. The piece of paper, still in his hand, seemed to burn his palm, as poker money had burned in his pocket; and he felt that he was but a pin hidden under a carpet and that Goyle could find him and thrust him back into obedience. The

Judge noticed the grip with which he held the slip of paper. "What have you there, George?" he asked.

"A—a—thing cut out of a newspaper." He opened his hand and the Judge looked at the slip of paper.

"But why did you grip it that way?" He took the cutting, smoothed it out, and, putting on his glasses, read it. "Ah," he said, handing it back, "that fellow. I have seen him in my sleep—last night. Tell him not to come here again."

"It has been some time since he was here."

"Don't apologize for him. Tell him that he must not enter this house again."

William came out and saw the Judge hand the cutting to Bodney. "Is it possible, John, that you believe in that nonsense, too?"

"I don't believe in anything," said the Judge.

"That's putting it rather strong," replied William. "That is to say, that when I tell you I elected Governors and Senators, you don't believe it." Bodney passed on, leaving the brothers walking up and down the hall, shoulder to shoulder.

"Did I say that I didn't believe you? What difference does it make anyway?"

"What difference does any man's record make?

If a man isn't proud of his record, what should he be proud of? You are proud of your decisions—they go to make up your record. I elected Governors, and—"

"Why didn't you elect yourself?"

"That's a nice way to come back at a man—your own brother. Haven't you heard me say that there is something higher than a desire for office? Hah, haven't you heard me say that?"

"Yes, there is something higher—the roof of the board of trade."

"John, that is an unfair thrust at my speculations. But, sir, at one time I could have closed out for millions. Do you understand, for millions."

"Why didn't you?"

"Now, just listen to that. Reproaches me for not being a money grabber, for not joining the robbers to crush the weaklings. I have suffered a good deal at your hands lately, but I didn't expect that stab. It wounds me here." He halted, and placed his hand on his breast. But he went in to breakfast and ate with the appetite of a man who, if wounded, must have marvelously recovered; he joked with Agnes about the preacher; he told her that it would be her duty to take care of his numerous slippers, presented by women. "And when you have a pound party at your house I will contribute a—"

"Senator," said Howard.

"Oh, so you have broken out, have you? I thought you were too deep in the study of French literature to pay any attention to such trifles. And you have got on a reddish necktie. You'll be an anarchist the first thing you know."

"He is going away, William," said Mrs. Elbridge, and the Judge did not look up. The sadness of her voice stirred William to repentance. "Going away? I don't see how we can get along without him. He and I joke, but we understand each other, don't we, Howard?"

"Perfectly, Uncle William; and when I open my ranch out West, you may look on it as your home."

"Thank you, my boy; but I don't care to go out there again. I was once a power there, but the country is now overrun with a lesser breed, and I am afraid that I might not get along with them. I want men, such as there used to be. Man will soon be a thing of the past. The scorcher is running over him—and I want to say right here, that if one of those fellows ever runs over me, he'll get a bullet just about the size of a—a—about the size of that." He held up his thumb and measured off the missile intended for the scorcher. "You hear what I say. Why, confound 'em, if they see a man, a real man, they bow their necks and make at him, but if one of them ever runs into me, the coroner will have a job."

Howard and Bodney went down town together and opened the office, as usual, for clients who did not come, and who, if they had come, would have shaken their heads and gone away.

"Howard," said Bodney, "I told you that I was financially ruined."

"Yes, I remember, but afterward you said that everything was all right, that your fit had passed. Has it come again?"

"It didn't go away. A sort of drunkenness made it appear so. The fact is, I am in need of ten dollars, to pay a man I owe. He keeps harassing me."

"I need every cent I've got, old man, but here's ten."

Bodney took the bank note and went out. The poker microbe was not so easily to be exterminated. It had suggested to Bodney that the only way to replace the money taken from the Judge's safe was to play poker. And, why not play? He might win—he had won once, and what the cards had done they would do again. He remembered the courtesies that had been shown him at the club, the congratulation of the man at the desk when he won and the sympathy when he lost. "Couldn't make 'em stick, eh? When a man gets the hands beaten you do, he's got to lose his money. There's nothing to it. But you'll get 'em yet—you play as good game as any of them." A man of sense could see that it was a losing game from the start, no matter how honestly conducted. And Bodney, going to the club before business put on its cheerful countenance, had seen them counting the swallowings of the ever hungry box, the rake-off, the unsatisfied maw. A fairly active game would average for the house at least eight dollars an hour, so that in the end every man must be a loser. He knew all this as the others knew it, but the microbe squirmed and made him itch.

He walked toward the Wexton Club, not in a rush, for he was still fighting. Speculation urged him to play one more time, and to realize during the game that it was the last. The hunger for play was surely dying; then, why kill it? why not let it die of its own accord? Then came the memory of nights of distress, the nervous sweat of anxiety in the street, scanning faces, looking for money. He turned aside, went into a hotel and sat down.

Two men were talking of a defaulter. "Yes, sir," said one of them, "everybody had confidence in him—the firm trusted him implicitly; but he embezzled and must go up for it." He mentioned the embezzler's name, and Bodney recognized it as that of a gentlemanly young fellow well known at the Wexton. He had come under an assumed name, but had thrown off this weak disguise, to indorse a check. So the players, who gossip among themselves, knew his real name, but addressed him as Jones. Bodney continued to listen. "I understand," said one of the men, "that the place where he went is a regular robbers' den." Bodney knew better than this; he knew that in the fairness, the courtesy, the good nature of the place lay its greatest danger. Men swore, it was true; cursed their luck and called upon a neighbor to testify to the fact that he had never seen such hands beaten; but for the most part, the atmosphere was genial, the talk bright and with a crispness rarely found in society. He resented this misrepresentation, and was even on the point of speaking when the men walked off. Soon afterward he went out, though not in the direction of the club; he circled round and round, like a deer, charmed by a snake; but after a time he saw the stairway, dusty and grim, rise before him. In the hall above, just as he was about to ring the bell, he thought of his short resources, only one ten dollar note, and he took out the crumpled paper and held it in his hand for a moment and looked at it, not to find the ten dollars, but the newspaper cutting. He started as if stung, stepped back and stood with his hand resting on the balustrade. The door opened and a man came out. Bodney spoke to him, and he halted. It was the offensive fellow with the white scar.

"How did you come out?"

The man opened both hands and raised them. He was not drunk now. He was sober and desperate. "They have ruined me," he said; "ruined me, and I don't know what in the name of God to do. I'll never play again as long as I live—I'd swear it on all the bibles in the world. Are you going to play?"

"I was thinking about it."

"I could have quit big winner. Say, have you got enough to stake me?" His eyes brightened, but the light went out when Bodney shook his head. "I've got just ten dollars."

"Then you won't last as long as a feather in hell." He went down the stairs, and Bodney continued to stand there, fighting against himself, with the newspaper cutting still in his hand. Suddenly, with his teeth set and both hands clenched, he ran down the stairs. At the door opening out upon the street he met the master of the game. "Won't you come back and eat with us?"

"No, I am in a hurry."

The master of the game was astonished. The idea of a poker player being in a hurry to get away from the game was almost new to him—and it was new to Bodney. But he hastened on, not daring to look back lest he might find some new temptation beckoning him to return. Passing beyond the circle wherein the lodestone seemed to draw the hardest, he felt, upon looking back, that he had escaped and was beyond pursuit. It was now eleven o'clock, and the victory must have been won at about ten minutes to eleven. He had cause to remember this afterward, on the following day, when he believed that the cause of this sudden strength had been revealed to him.

Howard was in the office when Bodney returned. "Well, did you pay your persistent creditor?"

"There was none. Here is your money; I don't need it now."

"But you will, so you'd better keep it."

"That's a fact, and I don't know how soon."

"But you say there was none."

"None. I'll explain sometime, but I can't now."

Howard did not pursue the subject further, for his mind was on his own affairs. He had settled upon taking his departure the next morning, and now he looked about the old room with a feeling of sadness. He had consulted another physician who knew his father well, and had been informed that the old man might improve rapidly in the absence of his son. This made the young man wince, but he had told the doctor that his father seemed to have an especial antipathy to him. "It is one of the freaks peculiar to diseased minds to turn upon one who has been nearest," said the physician. Howard had repeated this to his mother, and frequently she remarked it as a discovery of her own.

That evening when the young men went home there was a great hub-hub in the hall. William had just come in, covered with dust and was blowing like a hippopotamus. "If I live, I'll kill him; mind what I tell you."

"What's the trouble?" Howard asked. William had been knocked down by a scorcher.

CHAPTER XXII.

TOLD HIM GOOD-BYE.

At the breakfast table the next morning the Judge paid no attention to Howard, though he knew that his departure was to take place that day. He had striven to be genial when Mrs. Elbridge was present, and for a time had succeeded, but all effort was thrown off now.

Howard went to his room to make ready, and his mother went with him. The Judge was walking up and down in his office as they passed his door. Florence entered, and the Judge bowed to her.

"Are you going to tell Howard good-bye?" she asked.

"That's easy enough," he answered.

"He will come in here to see you before he goes."

"How do you know?"

"I know because it is not possible for him to prove so unnatural as—"

The Judge raised his hand. "Don't say it, please."

She stood looking at him. "Don't you think you ought to tell him why you have hardened your heart against him?"

"I shall tell him nothing."

"And is that the part of a true man? Is it not almost inhuman to let him suffer in ignorance?"

The Judge raised his hand and looked toward the door. "I tell you, it is to protect her. Can't you see?"

"It is well enough to protect her, but you ought to give him an opportunity to defend himself."

"There is no defense. Mind, your oath."

"Oh, I am sick of that," she said. "Every time I say a word in his behalf you remind me of a foolish vow. Judge, I am weary of this senseless and insane drama, seeing the others stumble about in the dark while you and I stand in the light. No, you do not stand in the light. I alone am in the light of truth; and if I did not think that the trip out West would be good for him, I would not let him go; I would stop him short with what you have told me and made me swear by the memory of my mother not to repeat. No wonder you put your hand to your head. It must ache. But, there, I won't reproach you."

He had sat down. She went to him and put her

hand on his shoulder. He looked up, and then looked down again. "I believe something is going to clear it all up one of these days," she said. He got up and resumed his walk. Howard's voice came down the hall: "Has the trunk gone yet?"

"I think he is coming," she said.

"Stay with me, Florence."

"No, you must face him, the injured, alone."

"I have not injured him; he has injured me."

She went out and the Judge stood there waiting for Howard. He came in, more serious now that everything had been made ready. "I am about to start for the West, sir," he said. "I can't stand it here any longer. You frown at me, and when I beg you to tell me—"

"How long do you expect to be gone?" the Judge interrupted.

"Till the day when I am to marry almost in secret, or when you send for me."

The Judge was walking up and down. He turned and replied. "I shall not send for you."

"Do you still deny us the right to be married in a church?"

"You shall never marry her at all with my sanction, and if you marry her without it, you marry out West or in there," he added, waving toward the drawing room. "There must be no guests."

"I should like to marry in my father's house, but on the prairie or in the woods will do as well; it makes no difference." He looked hard at his father, and, after a time, added: "I didn't think that a man could change so much—be so unnatural."

"None of that, sir!" the Judge exclaimed, turning upon him. "It is not for you to call me unnatural."

"Father, if I have committed a crime in your eye, why don't you tell me what it is?"

"In my eye! You must have studied long to frame that speech."

"But why don't you tell me?"

"Don't mock me, sir."

Howard looked at him, as if trying to study out something in his countenance, in his eye. "May I ask you something?"

"Why should you desire my permission since you would pay no attention to my refusal? What is it that you wish to ask?"

"May I ask if there has ever been any insanity in our family?"

The Judge started. "In our family—in my family there has been something worse than insanity."

Howard slowly nodded his head as if admitting a sad fact. "Yes, there has been the death of affection—in your family."

"Ah," cried the Judge, "the shrouding of a hope."

"The murder of a jovial spirit," said Howard.

"Don't shoot your poisonous arrows at me. Go on, away. Good-bye." He waved his hand. Howard turned toward the door, but halted, faced about and looked at the Judge with troubled tenderness. "Father, I don't know exactly where I am going, but out in the wilds somewhere to find a place for me and mine. I did not believe—couldn't have foreseen such a moment as this. It seems to me that my father is gone." He paused, and the Judge stood with his face turned away. "Shall I write to you?"

"No," said the Judge, without looking round.

Mrs. Elbridge came in and found them standing apart, the Judge still with his back toward Howard. "Howard," she said, "the cab is waiting. Judge, Howard is going away from us."

The old man turned slightly, looked at her, nodded his head, said "yes," and walked to the opposite side of the room. Mrs. Elbridge touched her forehead. "You must bear with him," she whispered. "You can see where the trouble lies."

"Yes, and it is a sorrowful thought. I can hardly believe it. And to think that he should select me as the object of his contempt."

"He will get over it soon and send for you," she said in a low voice. "A disordered mind turns against the loved one—nearly always." Then, advancing toward the old man, she said: "Judge, tell him good-bye."

"I have," replied the old man, standing with his face turned from her. She went to him and, touching his arm, said: "But not in your old way—not as you would have told him good-bye before—before you were ill."

"I am not ill," he said, without turning his eyes toward her. "I never was better in my life."

"But, tell him good-bye, please."

"I tell you I have!" he exclaimed, stamping upon the floor; and turning with his hand uplifted, he cried: "Can't you see—no, you cannot," he broke off, his hand shaking, and slowly falling to his side. "No, you cannot see, must not see. I beg your pardon for speaking so impatiently, but I am worried, Rachel; worried, and—"

"Yes, I know," she said, taking the arm which he had raised from under her gentle touch. "But, you must tell him good-bye."

The Judge struggled against her, though not with violence; the struggle, indeed, was more against himself. She led him toward Howard, who stood looking on, sorrowfully.

"Put your arm about him," she said to the Judge. "For me, please."

"For you," he said, and suffered her to put his arm on Howard's shoulder. She raised his other arm, and now he stood with both arms about the boy's neck.

"Good-bye, father," said Howard.

For a moment the old man's countenance was aglow with the light of love and sympathy; convulsively he pressed Howard to his bosom—but a horror seemed to seize him, the light of sympathy went out as if blown by a cold wind, and, stepping back, he said:

"There. Go. Not another word. Why do you continue to stand there gazing at me? Rachel, can't you take him away? I have told him good-bye to please you—now, why don't you oblige me by taking him away?"

"But, dear, have you no word for him?"

"Word, yes. Good-bye."

"No word of advice?"

"Advice! Don't mock me. Go away, please. Can't you see—no, you cannot, and why should I expect it? Now go."

"We are going," she said.

"Yes, but—I beg your pardon—but why don't you?"

She took Howard's arm and walked out, looking back as if she hoped that the Judge might repent and follow, but he did not; he resumed his walk up and down the room. Suddenly he turned. "Now, what are you doing, William?" The brother had entered and was turning over papers on the desk.

"I am looking for a slip of paper I dropped out of my pocket-book."

"You didn't leave anything here."

"That may be," said William, "but I don't know whether I did or not till I find out. A man never knows—"

"Some men never know," the Judge broke in, going over to the desk and taking a paper out of William's hand. "Go away, please." William stepped back, shocking himself from the storage battery of his dignity. "Oh, I can go, if that's what you want."

"That's what I want."

"It is? All right. John, I'll be hanged if I know what's the matter with you." The Judge was paying no attention. He was listening to a cab driving off from the door. "I say, sir, I'll be hanged if I know what's the matter with you."

"I heard what you said."

"I don't know whether you did or not. There's no living in the house with you. And last night, after I had been knocked down in the street—and I'm going to kill him if detectives can find him—last night when I merely intimated that something had taken place on the fourteenth of September, you—"

"William, are you going to begin all that over again?"

"I don't know what you mean by again. John, you talk in riddles. I can't for the life of me get at your meaning. Yes, sir, and last night you flew off like a jug handle when I told you that Carl Miller—"

"Oh, damn Carl Miller."

"That's all right. I don't care how much you damn him. He deserves it—broke a pair of boots for me and made 'em so kidney footed that I couldn't walk in 'em. But I am positive about that other date, John. It was the tenth."

The Judge looked at him, drew a long breath, and said: "William, you are an old fool."

"An old fool, John—old? Did you say old?"

"That is what I said. Old."

William sighed. "Then, that settles it. It isn't so bad to be simply a fool—for we may grow out of that as time goes on—but to be an old fool—John, I'll leave your house. I can't stand your abuse any longer. I am without means, broke, you might say, and I don't know which way to turn, except to turn my back on your ill-treatment of me. I may starve to death or be killed in the street or on some freight car, stealing a ride from misery to misery, but I am going."

"William, sit down and behave yourself."

"Never again will I sit down in your house. I have joked with you, I know, and have said a great many things that I didn't mean, but I am in deadly earnest this time. I am going away."

The Judge put his hand on William's shoulder. "Look at me," he said. "Don't leave me. I need you. I am mean, and I know it, but I beg of you not to leave me."

"Mean!" William cried. "Who the deuce said you were mean? Show the villain to me. Show him to me, I tell you."

"There, now, sit down; it is all right."

"No, sir, it is not all right, and it never will be till I find the scoundrel that called you mean. Was it Bradley? Tell me, and I'll choke him till his eyes pop out. Was it Bradley?"

The Judge smiled. "Bradley," said he, "is one of my props. He is the son of my old friend, and I think the world of him."

"Well, let him congratulate himself on his escape, for before the Lord I would choke him. It is all right, yes, sir—but, really, John, if I tell you earnestly it was on the tenth won't you believe—"

"Yes, yes; let it be the tenth."

"Let it be! Why, confound it, I tell you it was the tenth."

"All right. When you go out I wish you would tell Florence to come here."

William grunted. "Oh, I can go out. By the way, John, Howard asked me a pertinent question this morning. And it staggered me a little. He wanted to know whether there had ever been any insanity in our family."

The Judge showed signs of coming agitation, but he fought with himself as it was his custom to fight. "What did you tell him?"

"I lied, I told him no. John, do you remember the night when they came from the mad-house and told us children that father was dead?"

"Don't, William; don't. Please tell Florence to come here."

William went out and the Judge resumed his walk up and down the pathway of trouble. Yes, he did remember the night when they came from the mad-house, two men in a doctor's gig; he remembered the lamps on each side of the vehicle, eyes of a great bug, they seemed. But his father's malady had not come of inheritance, but of fever. But other men had fever and did not go mad. Could it be that he himself had been touched with the disease—touched in the eye with a vision? No, for there was Bodney. He had seen it. "My mind is sound, even in distress," he mused. "But wouldn't it have been better if I had talked to him kindly about his crime? I ought to have let him know that I saw him. No, his mother would have drawn it out of him—love sucking poison from a wound."

Florence entered the room, advanced a few paces, halted, and stood, looking at him. "Well, you sent for me and I am here."

"Yes, sit down, please."

"No, I thank you."

The Judge looked at her sorrowfully. "Did Howard tell you where he intends to go?"

Florence looked at him with a smile, but in the smile he saw bitterness. "Does it concern you?" she asked.

"I am not a brute, Florence."

"No," she said. "A brute is not unnatural."

"Don't, please. I am trying not to be unnatural. There can be a broken heart shielding a heart to keep it from breaking."

"You were a judge, a man of justice. And was it just to let him suffer in the dark? Was it right to lock your own lips and put a seal on mine. Judge, I ought to have told him in your presence."

"Don't say that."

"But I do say it. You presume upon what you are pleased to think is my strength of character. I am beginning to believe that I was weak instead of strong. Yes, I ought to have told him in your presence. I ought to have said: 'Your father, who has been a judge, has passed sentence upon you without giving you a hearing. He says you are a thief.'"

"Hush," said the Judge, in a loud whisper, motioning toward the door. "Don't talk that way to me. Ah, I have killed all the love you ever had for me."

"You have choked it and it is gasping."

"I am grieved—but it cannot be undone—the fingers are stiffened about your gasping love." He walked up and down for a time, and then turned again to her. "When you get a letter from him will you let me read it?"

"No. His heart will write to mine, and your eye would blur the words."

"Don't say that. I am not without a heart. I had a heart—it is broken." He walked off again, but turned quickly. "Florence, I sometimes wonder if my eye could have deceived me—could have lied to me."

She moved toward him, her hands uplifted, hope in her face. "A man's mind lies to him, and why not his eyes?" the Judge continued. Florence caught him by the arm and looked appealingly at him. "But your brother, Florence—your brother. He saw him, too."

"What!" she cried, stepping back. "Brother saw him! You didn't tell me that."

"I promised him I would not tell you."

"Ah, you break your promises and expect me to keep mine. I will go this moment and tell his mother."

He caught her arm and poured out a distressful imploration, a prayer. "I would rather you'd stab me," he said, concluding. "I would rather you'd kill us both. But I didn't swear, Florence. You have taken an oath."

"Judge, that is cowardly."

"Yes, it is. I am a coward—but only for her. A bitter word, Florence."

"Yes, forgive me. I didn't mean that. You are not a coward, but you are blind." He held forth his hands. She stepped back, shaking her head.

"All gone," said he, "all respect, all confidence. And you were my daughter."

"I was."

"In love and in duty," he said.

"In both," she replied. "In both, yes, and now love is gasping and duty has become a hard master." Suddenly she sprang toward him. "Brother saw him! I am just beginning to realize what you said. I don't believe it. His eyes lied, too."

"Oh, beautiful faith, it would move a mountain."

"It would pluck a mote from an eye. May I go now?"

"I am not on the bench to discharge or restrain you. But, just a moment. You feel that I am a tyrant. That could not have been possible with your former self. What is so cold as frozen gentleness? And now it is only through the frost-crusted windows that I can catch a glimpse of your other spirit."

"In the hall, yesterday," she said, "I thought that I heard a lurking echo of your old laughter."

He made a gesture of distress. "Don't remind me of it," he said.

"May I go?"

"Yes. But let me ask you one more favor. Don't tell your brother that I mentioned him."

"Another chain," she said.

CHAPTER XXIII.

THE LIGHT BREAKS.

The Judge turned and saw Bradley in the door. His appearance at any moment was not in the nature of a surprise. Agnes said that she expected him at most unexpected times. He no doubt regarded himself as a brave man, and perhaps he was; it required courage to be so timidly persistent.

"I hope I don't intrude," said the preacher.

"Oh, not at all. Come in."

"Miss Agnes is out for a walk, I understand," said Bradley, sitting down.

The Judge stood looking at him absent-mindedly. "Ah, yes, I suppose so. But I don't know why I suppose so. The truth is, I don't know anything about it. I beg your pardon, Bradley. I am—am greatly disturbed. The fact is, I hardly know what I am about. I am a mystery unto myself. I was just thinking of it as you came in. It does not seem possible for a man, with a mountain of sorrow upon his heart, to turn squarely about and speculate upon trivial things—to jest, if I may say so, and I must for it is a fact. I am glad you came."

"I am always delighted to come, Judge. Here I find the shade of a palm tree in a great desert of trade. And I came in the hope of finding you better."

"Better!" The Judge looked at him almost sternly. "Better, why I am not sick. What put that into your head, Bradley?"

"Why, I understood from what you have said that your health was not of the best."

"But it is of the best, I assure you. But I brood, yes, I brood, and that is worse than ill health—it is the ill health of the mind, the soul."

"I am afraid you work too hard."

"Um, work, I hardly know what that is. I am trying to rest, but it is like a man seeking sleep on a bed of thorns. Work is all right, for we can put it aside, but worry rides us till we are down, and then sits on our breast, waiting for us to get up."

William came in, shying a little upon seeing Bradley, but shook hands with him. "I am glad to see you looking so well, Mr. William," said the preacher.

"Oh, I'm a pine knot. Ain't I, John?"

The Judge looked at him inquiringly. "What did you say?"

"I said I was a pine knot."

"Did you?"

"Did I? Didn't I just say I did?"

"If you did, you did. That's all. But who accused you of not being a pine knot?"

Bradley chuckled, and William frowned at him; then, addressing himself to the Judge, the old fellow said: "You did. You disputed it. You call me a liar every time I open my mouth."

"William, you have often declared that you are not in the plot, but the first thing you know you may break into it."

"No, I won't!" William exclaimed, shaking his finger. "And I won't break into your intellectual atmosphere, either." He turned to Bradley. "Why, sir, John is a regular professor, browbeating his class. He expects everybody to talk book. I say, damn a book. I beg your pardon. It is the first time I ever said that in the presence of a preacher."

Bradley laughed. "It's all right, Mr. William, if you feel that way."

"Is it? Then, I say, damn a book. What I want is action."

"I subscribe to your doctrine concerning much of our literary output," said the preacher.

William was so delighted at this that he seized the preacher's hand and shook it with more of vigor than he was wont to put forth. "Good for you, Bradley. I am half inclined to come to hear you preach."

A twinkle in the Judge's eye showed that again he was playing in the midst of his sorrow. "You'd never get there, William. You could never settle on the date."

"Oh, you be confound, John. I have settled on more dates than you ever saw." He arose, went to the table and took up a pair of long shears. "Let me take these to my room, will you? I want to clip out something for my scrap-book."

"Oh, I thought you damned a book. No, sir, put those shears right down where you found them. You took my mucilage off yesterday and I had to go after it—down where you found them."

William put down the shears and looked angrily at the Judge. "Oh, I can put them down."

"Thank you."

"May I have a cigar, John?"

"Help yourself."

"Much obliged." He went to the desk, took up

a box of cigars and walked out unnoticed by the Judge, who had turned his back, following a strand of his sorrow, intertwined with a strand of humor, the two phases of himself which he could not comprehend. He walked slowly to the wall, and, turning, remarked, as he walked toward the preacher, "Bradley, I feel as one waiting for something—some shadow."

"I'm not a shadow," Agnes cried, skipping into the room. Bradley arose with a bow. "No, for shadows may be dark," he replied.

"Did you hear that, Mr. Judge? Did you hear him say that shadows may be dark? Of course, for if they were bright they wouldn't be shadows. May I sit here?" She sat on a corner of the long baize table swinging her feet, as if the music in her soul impelled her to dance, Bradley mused. "Why do you people stick in here all the time?" she went on. "Oh, I see," she added, lifting her hand with a piece of paper adhering to it. "You glue yourselves in here." She plucked off the paper, took out a handkerchief, a dainty bit of lace, and wiped her hand. "Have you just got here, Mr. Bradley? What's the news? Who's murdered on the West Side? They have murdered somebody every day since I came, first one side and then the other, and it's the West Side's turn today. Anybody killed today?"

"I don't know," Bradley replied, "but I hear that a prominent citizen was sand-bagged last night—in front of a church."

"Oh, for pity sake. And had he came out of a church fair? Did the robber get any money?"

"Bradley," said the Judge, "as William would say, she is putting it on you."

Bradley smiled, and said that it seemed so. Bodney stepped into the room, halted as if confused, and as Bradley got up to shake hands with him, hurriedly went out. Agnes spoke in an undertone to the preacher. "Mr. Bodney is worried, too. And it makes me awfully sorry to see the Judge so distressed at times. Can't you do something for him?"

"I can simply advise him not to worry, that's all."

"Beg him not to be so sad. I don't see how he can be. Everything is so bright."

The Judge went to the desk to get a cigar. "That rascal has taken every one of my cigars. Now, I've got to find him to recover my property." He went out, and they heard him calling William.

"They have to watch Mr. William all the time," said Agnes. "He carries off everything he can get his hands on. They say his room looks like a junk shop."

Bradley nodded in acknowledgment, and after a short silence, full of meditation, he said: "You seem still to enjoy your visit. And I hope you are not thinking of going home."

"Ah, ha, I am having a lovely time. Isn't it a nice place to visit. They make you feel so much at home, snap at each other if they want to, just as if you weren't here. That's the way for people to do; make you feel at home. But they are just as good as they can be, and their little spats are so full of fun to me, only it makes me sad to see the Judge worry. Yes, I am having a lovely time. I went to the vaudeville yesterday, and tomorrow I am going to your church."

"Oh, you are?" Bradley laughed.

"Ah, ha. Oh, do you know what I heard about you? I heard you were seen walking along the street with a drunken man."

"Yes, a friend of mine. And if a preacher shouldn't support a staggering brother, who should?"

"Oh, how human. I like you for that?"

"Do you?"

"Yes, I do."

"And for that alone?"

"Oh, no, I like you for that and for a good many other things. I think I could have lots of fun with you."

"Fun with me?" The preacher was thinking of a summer evening in Aldine Square, the music of the fountain, the sweetness of the flowers.

"Ah, ha. There's something about you that makes me feel like a little girl. And I dreamed that you took me by the hand and led me along."

"Agnes, let me lead you."

She slid off the corner of the table and stood with her hands flat together, like a delighted child, but suddenly she looked up with seriousness in her eyes. "But now you make me feel like a woman."

The Judge came in. Bradley spoke almost in a whisper. "But a woman might be led by a man." And then to the Judge he remarked, striving to hide his annoyance at the interruption: "I see you have recovered your property."

The Judge sat down on a chair near the table. "Yes, some of it. William is a good grabber, but he gives up after an argument, and there is some virtue in that."

"What was in the paper that worried Mr. Bodney so?" Agnes asked, speaking to the Judge.

"I don't know. Has anything worried him?"

"Yes, I saw him grabbing the paper as if he would tear it to pieces."

"Ball game, probably," said the Judge, and then looking at Agnes he added: "Nothing seems to bother you, little one."

"No, sir. I won't let it. When I am worried something jumps this way," she said, making an upward motion with her hands, indicating the sudden rise of spirits, "and the bother is gone."

The Judge spoke to Bradley. "The heart of youth jumps up and says boo to a trouble and frightens it away."

"Ah;" replied Bradley, "and couldn't an older heart learn to boo a trouble away?"

The Judge shook his head. "The old heart crouches, but cannot jump."

"Make it jump," Agnes cried. "Let me hear you laugh as you used to."

"The saints laugh with an old man," said Bradley.

"Don't," the Judge interposed, with a slow gesture. "Your roses are pretty, but you bring them to a funeral. No, I don't mean that. I mean that I am simply worried over a little matter, but I am getting better and will be all right pretty soon. I shall be my old self in a very short time." Bodney entered, and stood looking fixedly at the Judge. "What is it, George?"

Bodney nodded to Bradley and Agnes. "I beg your pardon, but I must see the Judge alone."

Bradley asked Agnes if she would accept of banishment with him. "Yes," she said. "Come on."

"It is not necessary," the Judge spoke up. "We can—"

"I beg your pardon," Bodney broke in, "but it is necessary."

"Of course it is," Agnes declared. "As Mr. William would say, we are not in the plot."

"No," said Bodney, bowing to her.

As they were going out, the Judge called to the preacher. "Don't go away without seeing me again, Bradley. I want you to spend the day with me."

Bodney leaned against the table, stepped off, came back, and stood looking down upon the Judge. The old man glanced up. "Well?"

It was some time before Bodney could speak. His words seemed dry in his mouth. At last he began: "I carried half of a heavy load. Something has thrown the other half on me, and I can't stand up under it—dispatch—railroad wreck—"

The Judge jumped out of his chair. "What!"

Bodney continued. "Yes. Goyle is dead."

"Oh, Goyle. I was afraid—where?"

"In Michigan, at fifteen minutes to eleven, yesterday. I have cause to note the time. The load—"

"Well, go ahead. But let me tell you now, George, you have no cause to regret the broken association. I deplore the man's death, of course, but I begun to feel that his influence upon you was bad. I had begun to dream about him, and to fear that he had a strange influence upon me. But go ahead."

"Half of it was crushing me, and I can't stand it all. I—"

"Why, what's the matter? What are you trying to tell. Go ahead."

"Judge, Goyle robbed the safe—Goyle and I—wait—I gave him the combination—he made up for Howard—I—"

The Judge seized the shears and raised them high above his head, his eyes fixed on Bodney's breast. Bodney did not flinch. The old man raised his eyes, to meet a steady gaze; and he stood with the shears high in his hand. He had uttered no outcry, no sound came from him, no sound that could have been heard beyond the door—only a low

The Judge seized the shears and raised them high above his head.

THE LIGHT BREAKS.

groan, like the moan of a fever-stricken man, turning over in his sleep.

"Kill me, Judge, I deserve it."

The shears fell from the old man's hand, and he dropped upon the chair, his arms upon the table and his face upon them.

"I wish you had struck me."

With a slight motion of the hand the Judge waved him off. Bodney continued: "For your heart there is a cure. There is none for mine. I was a fool, I was caught, I gambled, I couldn't quit, that snake held me, charmed me, hypnotized me. I knocked him down and he bled black on the floor, and I left him lying there, but I could not break loose from him."

The Judge waved him off. "Don't tempt me to look upon your face again."

Bodney did not move. "The old laugh that they have spoken so much about may return; old confidences and an old love will be restored, but there must be a wanderer that can never come back, a fool whom nature made weak. But I feel that if you would give me your hand—I am not deserving of it—but I feel that if I could once more touch that honorable hand, I could go forth an honest man. I would try."

The Judge slowly raised his head. Tears were in his eyes. He held forth his hand. Bodney grasped it, and—was gone.

CHAPTER XXIV.

SENT A MESSAGE.

William went to the office door and found it locked. This was so singular a happening that the old fellow stalked about the house, marveling over it and complaining against an innovation that shut a man out of an apartment that had served so long as a sort of public domain. It was like the closing of a park or a county road. Everyone laughed at him and he snorted. In the vocabulary of William's contempt, the snort was the strongest expression. "It is all right to laugh," said he, "but I want to tell you that there has got to be a change here." He returned to the office door and knocked upon it, but his knuckles aroused no heed within. He could hear the Judge walking up and down. Bodney had been gone nearly half an hour. But the Judge had not noted the time. To him, life was but a conflicting, mental eternity, and he was in the whirling midst of it. For a long time he sat with his head on the table, one arm stretched out before him, the other hanging limp; then he staggered about the room, and then sat down with his head in his hands. To the eye turned inward all was black, till gradually a light appeared, seeming softly to shine upon a hideous shape, crouching in a dark corner. He gazed upon it, and it spoke, shrinking further back from the soft light. "I am your injustice," it said. He got up, raised a window, and stood looking out upon the sunlight in the street. But he shivered as if with cold, and his lips moved as if he were talking and swallowing his words down into deep silence. A gladness began to form in his heart. His son was innocent, but in that innocence there was a reproach. He had been unnatural as a father, and might he not many a time have been unjust as a judge? He acknowledged to himself that he must have decided in favor of error while on the bench. His retirement was a sort of unconscious justice. He realized that his mind had not been sound. He had felt a coming weakness. But now he felt a coming strength. The trial through which he had passed must have served as a test. It was to restore or ruin his mental life. But why should there have been such a test, and why should the innocent have suffered? It would not do to reason, and he banished the test idea, fighting it off. Still, he acknowledged that his mind had sickened and that now it was gaining strength. He remembered his frivolity and loathed it, his jokes with William at a time when his heart was heavy and swollen. "Unnatural as a father and inconsistent as a man," he muttered. "But who is to judge of man's naturalness? One kink in the mind and the entire world is changed." William knocked again, and now the Judge opened the door. The old fellow looked at his brother and exclaimed:

"Why, what has happened, John?"

"Nothing, except that I have been really ill. But I am almost recovered. My mind has passed through a sort of crisis, William. I can now look back and see that I was not right. My present strength tells me of my former weakness. I am soon to be entirely well."

"Well, I am glad to hear that. It is particularly gratifying to me. And I suppose that you are, or, at least, soon will be, willing to concede that I am sometimes correct with regards to my dates."

"Yes, but we won't mention that. It is of no importance."

"What! No importance? Take care, John, you'll get back where you were, for when a man says that a date is of no importance, he's in danger."

"William, I want you to do me a favor. I am almost afraid to trust myself to go out just now. Wait a moment." He went to his desk, found a telegraph blank, and upon it wrote the following message: "The light has broken. Come back at once." William read the words and looked at him. "Go to the station," said the Judge, "and send this to Howard, in care of the conductor. It is not a secret, mind you, but don't stay to show it. They would delay you with puzzling over it."

"All right, I'll jump into a cab and go right over. I know the station. It's only a few blocks from here. He didn't go all the way down town. I heard him tell his mother. By the way," William added, "I found one of Howard's French books—"

"Put it back where you found it."

"What, you haven't flopped, have you?"

"I don't know what you mean."

"Why, you said that French literature was the—"

"It is the civilizing force of the modern world. Go on, please. Just a moment. Tell Florence that I wish to see her."

When Florence came in her face was radiant. William had spread the news of Howard's recall. "Ah," said the Judge, "you know that I have sent for him."

"Yes, father," she replied, going up to him with outstretched hands. He took her in his arms and kissed her. "What has happened?" she asked.

"The atmosphere is cleared, my dear."

"But, what cleared it?"

"The truth. You were right. I saw a vision."

She looked at him. "But what was it that brother saw?"

"Ah," said the old man, shaking his head, "you are shrewd. You are not willing to let it pass. Florence, we both saw Goyle disguised with his devilish art as Howard."

She gazed at him. "Is that all?"

"All? Is not that enough for us to know, my child?"

"But, why did brother happen to lead you into the office just at that time?"

"There, I have told enough; and what I have told you must not repeat. If there is anything to come, Howard may tell you, but my wife must never know that I have been so weak and unnatural a father."

"But she can see that something must have occurred to change your bearing toward Howard. Mr. William has told her that you have sent for him, and she is in her room with tears of joy in her eyes."

"Florence, I am striving to be calm, the master of myself. I don't deserve to be happy—not yet. How could I have been so blind? And how at times could I have indulged in levity with such a sorrow upon my heart?"

"It was the truth, father, striving to break through."

He nodded his head. "Yes, and now we must tell her something. Ah, tell her that a man came and brought me word that my brother is not dead. Keep her from coming to me with any sort of demonstration. I can't stand it. I must recall my old self and become gradually accustomed to it. I must realize that it was all a dream and that it is passing away. Tomorrow, with Howard, we may make a joke of it."

"It will never be a joke with me."

"No, my child, I did not mean that. It was a nightmare—a breath-shape breathed upon us by the devil while we slept. But we are awake now, and God's sun shines. Go to her and tell her that my brother is not dead."

"I will. But, father, do you realize how resourceful you have made me—how replete with falsehood? And must I not go into the closet and pray for forgiveness?"

"It was done for love, my dear; and love, which is the soul of all up yonder, has forgiven already."

Florence and Mrs. Elbridge entered the drawing room. "Who brought that news that his brother was not dead?" Mrs. Elbridge asked.

"A man. He was in a great hurry to catch a train and could not stop long. He brought direct word from Mr. Henry himself."

"Then there can be no doubt about it."

"No. And I did not believe it in the first place."

"Who is in there with him?"

"I think Agnes and the preacher have just gone in."

"This is a happy day," said Mrs. Elbridge, looking toward the door.

"A day when falsehood may be told, but when truth is revealed," Florence replied. "It is one of God's days."

"All days are His, my dear."

Florence slowly shook her head. "No, not all."

The Judge came in. He put his arms about Mrs. Elbridge. "Rachel," he said, "you shall never see my face gloomy again. I will go laughing down into green old age, into the very moss of time." He motioned toward the office. "In there is a beautiful picture of sweet distress."

Mrs. Elbridge looked upon him with a trembling lip. "But, my dear, it is not more beautiful than the fact that you sent for your son and that you yourself have come back to us all."

The Judge smiled. Florence could see that he was growing stronger, that his mind was clearing. "He returns like a lost child suddenly finding the path home," she said.

"Faith has its wisdom and its reward," replied the Judge, looking at her. "In the days of the New Testament, you would have been one of the followers. You would have wiped His feet with your hair." And, looking at his watch, he added: "I wonder why William doesn't come back."

"It is not time," Mrs. Elbridge replied, glancing at the clock.

"The minutes are hours, but clearing and strengthening hours," said the Judge. He turned about and began to walk up and down the room, with all the simpleness of his nature in his face. He did not look like a man who had sat in judgment upon the actions of men. His heart had cried for pardon, and a belief that it had come lighted his countenance. A man who has been shrewd in the affairs of the world, sharp in practice, suspicious, sometimes becomes simple and trustful in the love of a grandchild. And at this time, the Judge might have reminded one of such a man.

Mrs. Elbridge stood in the door looking down the hall. The Judge halted to speak to Florence. "Forgiveness," said he, "is the essense of all that is noble in life. And do you forgive me?"

"Yes," she said. "And I hope that I shall be forgiven all the falsehoods I have been forced to tell."

"They were for her, Florence, and there is a virtue in an untruth that shields a heart." He moved closer to her and added: "I wonder at your strength and marvel at my weakness."

"You were groping in the dark. It was not your fault, but your nature."

"And you are my daughter again."

"Yes," said Florence, "in love and in duty."

Mrs. Elbridge went out. The Judge and Florence sat down to wait for William. He was a sort of way-station which must be reached before they could arrive at Howard. The Judge told her of the darkness through which he had passed, throwing new light upon it, as if she had not seen it, as she stood by, holding a torch. He spoke of Goyle, of his strange power; he told her of the newspaper cutting that gave account of his mind-reading, and finally he told her of Bodney's confession. She was prepared, and showed no agitation. But there was grief on her face. Then he told her that he could not find it in his heart to condemn him. "In your own words, Florence, it was not his fault, but his nature. I will take him back, and not even Howard must know of his part in—in my darkness."

"Howard ought to know everything," she said.

"But not now, my dear; by degrees, as he shall be able to bear it. He is generous, and I believe he will forgive."

Mrs. Elbridge returned and stood in the door. "Here comes William," she said. The Judge arose. William came in puffing. "We were looking for you," said Mrs. Elbridge.

"Well, now," replied the old fellow, "you don't have to look long for me, I'll tell you that. I made the driver whip his horses all the way there and back."

"And are you sure that your message caught the train?" said the Judge.

"Oh, I always fetch 'em whenever I go after 'em."

"Are you sure you sent it all right?" the Judge asked.

"John, I thought you'd get well. But, sir, you

exhibit the most alarming sign of sickness I have ever seen in you. Sure I sent it all right! What other way do I ever do a thing? Of course I sent it all right. The train wasn't far out, and there's one back every few minutes."

"It seems that he has been gone a year instead of two hours," said the Judge.

Florence smiled at him. "And are we to be married in secret?" she asked, speaking low.

"My dear, that shall be as you please. I have only one wish—that it shall be one of the happiest days of my life, and I believe that it will be."

"What day of the month is this?" William asked.

"The fifth," the Judge answered.

"Are you sure?"

"I am sure it is not the tenth of June, sixty-three," said the Judge, and was in deep regret at his levity at such a time, when his wife spoke up, "Judge, please don't get him started."

"Started!" William snorted. "Now—now, that's good. A man races all the way to the station and back, and they talk about getting him started." Suddenly he thrust his hands into his pockets and stood staring at the wall. "Well, if that don't beat anything I ever saw."

"What is the trouble?" the Judge asked.

"Why, I dated that telegram the fourth."

"You did!" Mrs. Elbridge cried. The Judge looked hard at his brother. "It won't make any difference," said Florence. "He will know that it was a mistake."

"He will undoubtedly know who sent it," the Judge added.

"I wonder why Mr. Bradley and Agnes stay in that dingy place," said Mrs. Elbridge, always anxious to change the talk from William's dates.

"The place may be dingy," replied the Judge, "but there are no cobwebs hanging from the rafters in the abode of love."

"Judge!" she said, giving him a smiling frown.

"To some eyes," remarked Florence, half musingly, "there may be cobwebs hanging from the rafters in love's abode, but to love they are strands of gold."

"Let us go out and watch for his coming," said Mrs. Elbridge, taking Florence by the arm. They went out, leaving William staring at the Judge.

"By the way, what's this I happened to hear about brother Henry being dead? I didn't know he was dead till he wasn't."

"You didn't?"

"I mean I heard the news of his death and the

contradiction about the same time. Why did you keep it from me?"

"Oh, I knew there wasn't any truth in the report, and there wasn't anything to be gained by telling you."

"Anything to be gained. Do you only tell a man a thing when there is something to be gained by it?"

The Judge looked at the clock and then at his watch. "He ought to be here pretty soon. I want everybody to keep away from me. I want to see him first alone—in here."

"But what's all this mystery about? I'll be hanged if you haven't put my light under a bushel."

"No, William, it is my light that has been under a bushel."

"Everything may be all right, John, but I don't understand it. There was something I wanted to say. Yes. In case I forget it, tell him the date was a mistake."

"You won't forget it, William. You never forget a mistaken date."

"There you go again. Can't a man make a request?"

"I believe a man can, William."

"You don't believe anything of the sort, and you

know it. But I won't be left in the dark. I refuse to stumble in ignorance." He started toward the door.

"What are you going to do?"

"I am going to get the morning paper and settle that date."

"All right," said the Judge, as William went out. "And tell them out there that I must see him here alone. Don't forget that." He walked up and down the room and then stood at the door. "Do you see anything of him yet?" he called to his wife.

"Not yet. It isn't time. But here's a cab. It's going to stop—no, it's gone on."

"Let me get there," said the Judge, as if the others were responsible for the fact that the cab had not halted and put Howard down at the door. A moment after he went out Bradley and Agnes entered the room. "They are gone to watch for him. Shall we go, too?" the girl asked, looking at him with a mischievous quiz in her eyes.

"No, let us stop here a moment. Strange, isn't it, his going away and coming back so soon?"

They sat on a sofa, looking at each other as if new interests were constantly springing up.

"We have talked all over the house," she said. "I feel as if I have been on an excursion. Yes, it is strange. Don't you think they have quarreled?"

"Perhaps—but it will bring them closer together."

"Yes," she said, "but I wouldn't like to quarrel just to be brought closer together. I wonder why Mr. Bodney went away, too."

"And you ask?"

"Yes, didn't you hear me? I heard him muttering as he went out. And I understood him to say that he wasn't coming back any more."

"I thought you knew why he went."

"Thought I did? How was I to know?"

"I could not help but think—"

"What did you think?" she broke in.

"That he had asked you to be his wife and—"

"Oh, he never thought of such a thing."

"And if he should?"

"I'd tell him no, of course."

"You may have to say yes sometime, Agnes."

She looked down. "I won't have to—but I may."

"Agnes, do you know what love is?"

"What a question. Of course I do."

"What is it?"

"Oh, it's er—er—don't you know what it is?"

"Yes, Agnes, it is a glorious defeat of the heart."

"Oh, I don't think so. It's more a victory than a defeat."

SENT A MESSAGE.

"No, the heart surrenders." They heard the Judge exclaim, "No, it is not going to stop."

"Agnes, did your heart ever surrender?"

"You must not ask me that."

"Why not? Did your heart ever fight till it was so tired that it had to give up—surrender?"

"You mustn't ask me that. You'll make me cry." She hid her eyes.

"In sorrow, Agnes?"

"No—no, in happiness."

He put his arms about her, kissed her, pouring forth his dream of the fountain and the evening in summer. The Judge startled them. "Don't let me disturb your tableau," he said, laughing, "but I must see my son in here alone, not in the office where—where the safe is."

"Come," said Bradley, taking Agnes by the hand, "Let us watch with them."

As they arose the Judge looked at Agnes. "Ah, I see happiness in your face, little one. Keep it there, Bradley, for it is God-given." He took the preacher's hand. "God bless you, Bradley. You are a good fellow."

"Don't call him fellow, Mr. Judge," said the girl, pretending to pout.

"Yes, fellow," Bradley replied. "It is closer to the weakness of man."

"Closer to his heart, Bradley," said the Judge.

"Yes," said Bradley, and then he spoke to Agnes. "Come with me."

"Anywhere with you," she replied, taking his arm and looking up into his face. They passed out, and the Judge stood, waiting. William appeared at the door. "It's all right now, John."

"What's all right?"

"That date—the one that caused so much trouble one night. It was on the tenth."

"Is it finally settled?" the Judge asked, listening.

"Yes, sir, finally, and nothing can throw me off. Here comes Howard." The Judge motioned, and William withdrew. Howard's footsteps were heard. The old man stood with his face turned from the door, striving to master himself. He felt that surely he should break down. Howard stepped into the room. "Father," he said. The Judge turned, and, perfectly calm, held forth his hand. Howard grasped it. "My son, let us be masters of ourselves. Let us be strong, for you will have need of strength. I have something to tell you."

"No," Howard replied. "You have nothing to tell. George met me at the station and told me. I have forgiven him I know how he has suffered. I have seen his struggles. He must not be sent away.

I have brought him back with me. He is out there."

"Howard," said the old man, "you are a noble fellow."

Howard stepped to the door and called Bodney. When he entered the Judge said: "George, I am going to rent an office in a modern building. That old place is worn out. We are going to start new. Ah, come in, Florence."

"I have simply come to tell you that dinner is ready," she said, with tears in her eyes.

"Yes," said the Judge. "Come, boys." Florence led the way, looking back, smiling, and the old man went out between Bodney and Howard, with his hands resting on their shoulders. In the hall stood Agnes, the preacher and William. The preacher was speaking. "If there were but one word to express all the qualities of God, I should select the word forgiveness," he said.

THE END.

www.ingramcontent.com/pod-product-compliance
Lightning Source LLC
Chambersburg PA
CBHW022112230426
43672CB00008B/1351